Laboratory Manual
Of
Glassblowing

Watchmaker Publishing

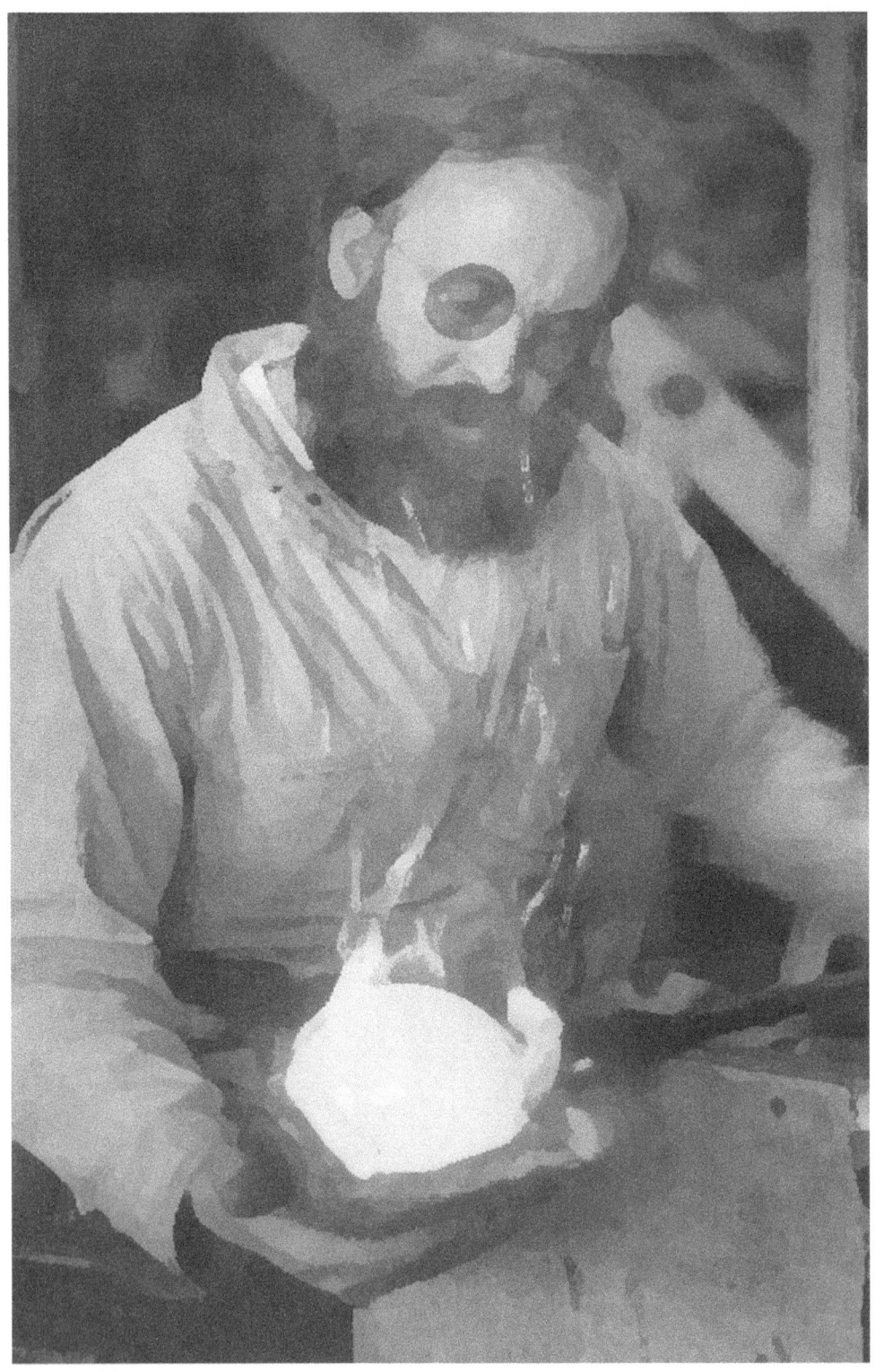

Laboratory Manual
Of
Glassblowing

By
Francis C. Frary, Ph.D.

First Edition
Third Impression

Watchmaker Publishing
1914

Copyright © 2009 Watchmaker Pub

ISBN 1-60386-262-5

Digitalized by
Watchmaker Publishing
All Rights Reserved

PREFACE

The purpose of this little book is to provide a clear and detailed discussion of the elements of glass-blowing. Many laboratories in this country, especially in the west, are located a long way from any professional glass-blower, and the time and money spent in shipping broken apparatus several hundred miles to be mended could often be saved if some of the laboratory force could seal on a new stop-cock, replace a broken tube, or make some temporary repairs. Many men in physical or chemical laboratories have occasion to modify some piece of apparatus designed perhaps for other uses, or to design new apparatus. To such also, the ability to perform some of the operations herein described may be very valuable.

No originality is claimed for the methods here described. They are those which the author has found most suitable and convenient in his own work, and most easily learned by students. The aim has been to describe each operation in such detail that a beginner can follow the process without help and, with practice, attain satisfactory results. It is, however, much easier to perform any of the operations described, after seeing some one else perform it correctly; since the temperature, the exact time to begin blowing the glass, and many other little details are very difficult to obtain from a description.

It has not been thought worth while to describe the process of making stop-cocks, thermometers, vacuum tubes, etc., as such things can be purchased more cheaply and of much better quality than any amateur can make unless he is willing to spend a very large amount of time in practice. For similar reasons the manipulation of quartz glass has been omitted.

The author will be grateful for all suggestions and criticisms tending to improve the methods presented If some of them appear to be given in excessive detail, the reader will remember that many things which are obvious to the experienced worker are not so to the beginner, and that it is the little details in the manipulation which often spell success or failure in glass-blowing.

F. C. F.

MINNEAPOLIS, MINN.,
January, 1914.

CONTENTS

	PAGE
PREFACE	v

CHAPTER I

MATERIALS AND APPARATUS 1
    Varieties and defects of glass—Devitrification—Annealing glass—Blowpipe and bellows—Light—Arrangement of exercises.

CHAPTER II

GENERAL OPERATIONS 7
    Cutting, bending, constricting and flanging the tubing—Methods of rotation and blowing.

CHAPTER III

ELEMENTARY EXERCISES 16
    Joining two pieces of tubing of the same diameter—The "tee" tube—Joining two tubes of different diameters—Blowing bulbs.

CHAPTER IV

ADVANCED EXERCISES 35
    Sealing a tube through another tube: The gas-washing tube, suction pump, and Kjeldahl trap.

CHAPTER V

MODIFIED METHODS AND SPECIAL OPERATIONS 43
    Capillary tubing—Glass rod—Mending stopcocks—Closed circuits of tubing—Spirals—Ground joints—Sealing in platinum wire—Sealing vacuum tubes—Closed tubes for heating under pressure.

INDEX 59

Recipes For Flint Glass Making   61

LABORATORY MANUAL OF GLASS-BLOWING

CHAPTER I

Materials and Apparatus

One of the most important factors in the success of any piece of glass-blowing is the glass employed. As is well known, there are two general varieties of glass: Lead glass and soda glass. Formerly much apparatus was made of lead glass, but at present it is very seldom met with, except in the little drops of special glass used to seal platinum wires into the larger sizes of tubes. Lead glass is softer and more readily fusible than soda glass, but has the disagreeable property of growing black in a few seconds unless worked in a strong oxidizing flame. This may be prevented by using a "hissing" flame, with a large excess of air, and working in the extreme end of the flame; or the black lead formed may thus be reoxidized, and the glass restored to its original clearness.

Almost all the soft glass on the market is a soda glass, although sometimes part of the soda is replaced by potash. Most of the hard glass appears to be a potash glass. The following qualities are desirable in a glass for ordinary working: (1) moderately low working temperature, (2) freedom from air bubbles, striations and irregularities, (3) proper composition, so that the glass will not devitrify or crystallize while being handled at its working temperature, (4) ability to withstand rapid heating without cracking.

The working temperature of different samples of so-called "soft glass" varies a good deal, and is best determined by trial. The glass should become almost soft enough for blowing in a flame that still shows a little yellow near the tip, so that at the highest temperature of the flame it may flow fairly freely and thus easily eliminate irregularities in thickness. If the glass is too hard, the shrinking of the glass, collection of material for a bulb, and in fact most of the working processes will be slower, and the glass will not stay at its working temperature long enough after its removal from the flame to permit it to be properly blown.

Air bubbles in the original batch of glass are drawn out into long hair-like tubes during the process of manufacture. When such tubing is worked, the walls of these microscopic tubes collapse in spots, and the air thus enclosed will often collect as a small bubble in the wall, thus weakening it. Irregularities are of various kinds. Some of the larger sizes of thin-walled tubing often have one half of their walls much thicker than the other, and such tubing should only be used for the simplest work. Some tubing has occasional knots or lumps of unfused material. The rest of the tube is usually all right, but often the defective part must be cut out. The presence of striations running along the tube is generally an indication of hard, inferior glass. Crookedness and non-uniformity of diameter are troublesome only when long pieces must be used.

Devitrification is one of the worst faults glass can possibly have. It is especially common in old glass, and in glass which has contained acids. It seems to be of two sorts. One variety manifests itself on the surface of the glass before it reaches its working temperature, but if the glass be heated to the highest temperature of the flame it will disappear except in the portion at the edge of the heated part. The glass seems to work all right, but an ugly crystallized ring is left at the edge of the portion heated. This kind appears most frequently in old glass which was originally of good quality, but has in time been superficially altered, probably by the loss of alkalies. The other variety of devitrification does not appear when the glass is first heated; but after it has been maintained at or above its working temperature for a longer or shorter time, it will be noticed that the outer surface has lost its smoothness, and appears to be covered with minute wrinkles. It will also be found that the glass has become harder, so that it becomes impossible to work it easily. Further heating only makes the matter worse, as does the use of a higher temperature from the start. In fact it will often be found that a piece of comparatively soft glass which devitrifies almost at once in a "hissing" flame can be worked without serious difficulty if care be taken to use a flame still decidedly tinged with yellow. Even good glass will begin to devitrify in this way if heated too long at the highest temperature of the flame, so care should always be taken (1) *to reduce the time of heating of any spot of glass to a minimum; i.e.*, get the desired result at the first attempt, if possible, or at least with the minimum of reheating and "doctoring," and (2) *avoid keeping the glass at the highest temperature of the flame any longer than necessary.* This may be accomplished by doing all heating, shrinking, etc., of the glass in a flame more or less tinged with yellow, and only raising the temperature to the highest point when ready to blow the glass. This kind of devitrification is apparently due to volatilization of the alkalies from the glass in the flame, and it is said that it can be partly remedied or prevented by holding a swab of cotton saturated with a strong solution of common salt in the flame from time to time as the glass is heated.

The toughness of glass, *i.e.*, its ability to withstand

variations of temperature, depends on its composition and the care taken in its annealing. In general, large pieces of glass should be heated very slowly in the smoky flame, and the larger the diameter of the tube the greater the length which must be kept warm to prevent cracking. All large pieces should be carefully heated over their whole circumference to the point where the soot deposit burns off, before being finally cooled. After being thus heated they are cooled in a large smoky flame until well coated with soot, then the flame is gradually reduced in size and the object finally cooled in the hot air above it until it will not set fire to cotton. If thought necessary, it may then be well wrapped in cotton and allowed to cool in the air. If not properly annealed the place heated may crack spontaneously when cold, and it is quite certain to crack if it is reheated later.

Next in importance to the glass are the blow-pipe and the bellows. Any good blast lamp, such as is ordinarily used in a chemical laboratory for the ignition of precipitates, will be satisfactory; provided it gives a smooth regular flame of sufficient size for the work in hand, and when turned down will give a sharp-pointed flame with well-defined parts. Where gas is not available, an ordinary gasoline blow-torch does very well for all operations requiring a large flame, and a mouth blow-pipe arranged to blow through a kerosene flame does well for a small flame. Several dealers make blow-torches for oil or alcohol which are arranged to give a small well-defined flame, and they would doubtless be very satisfactory for glass-work. Any good bellows will be satisfactory if it does not leak and will give a steady supply of air under sufficient pressure for the maximum size of flame given by the lamp used. A bellows with a leaky valve will give a pulsating flame which is very annoying and makes good work very difficult. When compressed air is available it can be used, but if possible it should be arranged so that the supply can be controlled by the foot, as both hands are usually needed to hold the work. For the same reason the supply of air is usually regulated by varying the rate of operation of the bellows, rather than by adjusting the valve of the blast-lamp. On the other hand, it will be found best to always adjust the flow of the gas by means of the cock on the lamp, rather than that at the supply pipe. The operator must have complete control over the flame, and be able to change its size and character at short notice without giving the work a chance to cool, and often without ceasing to support it with both hands.

Glass-blowing should be done in a good light, but preferably not in direct sunlight. The operator should be seated in a chair or on a stool of such a height that when working he may comfortably rest one or both elbows on the table. The comfort of the operator has a decided influence on the character of his work; especially in the case of a beginner, who often defeats his purpose by assuming uncomfortable and strained positions. Steadiness and exact control of both hands are essential in most operations; any uncomfortable or strained position tires the muscles and weakens the control of the operator over them.

In the arrangement of the exercises here presented, several factors have been considered. It is important that the first exercises be simple, although not necessarily the simplest, and they should teach the fundamental operations which will be used and amplified later. They should in themselves be things which are of importance and commonly used in glass-work, and they should be so arranged that the fundamental points, such as the rotation of glass, the proper temperature, blowing and shrinking the glass may be learned with a minimum expenditure of time, glass and gas. It is therefore recommended that the beginner take them up in the order given, at least as far as No. 7, and that each be mastered before attempting the next. The beginner should not leave the first exercise, for example, until he can join together two pieces of tubing so that they form one piece of substantially uniform inner and outer diameter, and without thick or thin spots. From two to four practice periods of two hours each should suffice for this. This chapter and the following one should also be frequently read over, as many of the points discussed will not be understood at first and many of the manipulations described will not be necessary in the simpler exercises.

CHAPTER II

General Operations

Cutting the Glass.—For this purpose a "glass-knife" is preferred to a file, if the glass is cold: if it is hot a file must always be used, and its edge slightly moistened to prevent drawing the temper. The glass-knife is simply a flat piece of hard steel, with the edges ground sharp on an emery wheel. The bevel of the edge should be from 30 to 60 degrees. An old flat file can easily be ground into a suitable knife. The glass-knife makes a narrower scratch than the file but appears more likely to start the minute crack which is to cause the tube to break at that point, and the break is more likely to give a good square end. The scratch should be made by passing part of the knife or file once across the glass, never by "sawing" the tool back and forth. This latter procedure dulls the tool very quickly.

In breaking a piece of glass tubing, many persons forget that it is necessary to *pull* the ends apart, as well as to bend the tube very *slightly* in such a direction as to open up the minute crack started in the scratch. Care in breaking the tube is essential, as it is impossible to do as good work with uneven ends as with square ones.

When tubing of large diameter or thin wall is to be cut, it is often better not to attempt to break it in the usual way, but to heat a very small globule of glass (1/16 to 1/8 inch diameter) to red heat, and touch it to the scratch. This will usually start the crack around the tube; if it has not proceeded far enough, or has not gone in the desired direction, it may be led along with a hot point of glass. This is put a little beyond the end of the crack, and as the latter grows out toward it, moved along the path where the crack is desired. This point of glass is also very useful in breaking off very short ends of tubes, where there is not room to get a firm enough hold and sufficient leverage to break the tube in the ordinary way, and for breaking tubes attached to large or heavy objects, which would be likely to make trouble if treated in the ordinary way.

Another way of cutting large tubing, especially if it has rather thick walls, is to make a scratch in the usual way, and then turn on the smallest and sharpest possible flame of the blast lamp. The tube is next taken in both hands and held horizontally above the flame so that the scratch is exactly over it. The tubing is now rotated rapidly about its axis, and lowered so that the flame is just tangent to its lower side. After about ten seconds of heating, it is removed from the flame and the hot portion quickly breathed upon, when it will generally crack apart very nicely. Care must be taken to hold the tube at right angles to the flame during the heating, and to rotate it so that only a narrow strip of the circumference is heated, and the scratch should be in the center of this heated strip. By this means tubing as large as two inches in diameter is readily broken.

Griffin's glass cutter, which contains a hardened steel wheel, like that on any ordinary window-glass cutter, and a device by which this can be made to make a true cut clear around the tube, is a very handy article, especially for large tubing, and may be obtained from any dealers in chemical apparatus.

Bending Glass.—Inasmuch as this is one of the commonest operations in the laboratory, it is assumed that the reader knows how to perform it. However, it should be noted that in order to obtain the best results a broad (fish-tail burner) flame should generally be used, and the tube rotated on its axis during the heating, and allowed to bend mostly by its own weight. If large tubing is to be bent, one end must be stoppered and great care used. Whenever the tube shows signs of collapsing or becoming deformed, it must be gently blown out into shape, heating the desired spot locally if necessary. A blast-lamp is likely to be more useful here than the fish-tail burner.

Drawing Out a Tube.—Most students learn this the first day of their laboratory work in chemistry, but few take pains to do it well. The tube should be heated in the flame of a Bunsen burner, or blast lamp (preferably the latter) until it is very soft. During this time it must be continuously rotated about its axis, and so held that the edges of the heated zone are sharply defined; *i.e.*, it should not be allowed to move back and forth along its own axis. When so hot that it cannot longer be held in shape, the tube is removed from the flame, and the ends slowly and regularly drawn apart, *continuing the rotation of the tube about its axis*. By regulating the rate of drawing and the length of tube heated, the desired length and diameter of capillary may be obtained. The tube should always be rotated and kept in a straight line until the glass has set, so that the capillary may have the same axis as the main tube. This capillary or "tail" is often a very necessary handle in glass-blowing, and if it is not straight and true, will continually make trouble.

In drawing out very large tubing, say from one to two inches in diameter, it is often necessary to draw the tube *in the flame*, proceeding very slowly and at a lower temperature than would be used with small tubing. This is partly on account of the difficulty of heating large tubing uniformly to a high temperature, and partly in order to prevent making the conical part of the tube too thin for subsequent operations.

Constricting a Tube.—Where a constriction is to be made in a tube, the above method must be modified, as the strength of the tube must be maintained, and the constricted portion is usually short. Small tubes are often constricted without materially changing their outside diameter, by a process of thickening the walls. The tube is heated before the blast lamp, rotating it about its axis as later described, and as it softens is gradually pushed together so as to thicken the walls at the heated point, as in *a*, Fig. 1. When this operation has proceeded far enough, the tube is removed from the flame, and the ends cautiously and gently drawn apart, continuing the rotation of the tube about its axis and taking care not to draw too rapidly at first. The resulting tube should have a uniform exterior diameter, as shown in *b*, Fig. 1.

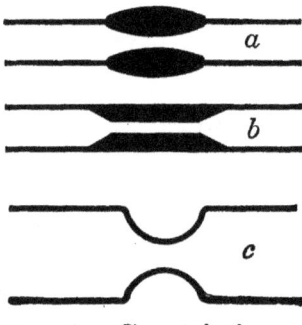

Fig. 1.—Constricting a tube.

This method of constriction is not suited to tubes much over 1/4 inch in diameter, since the mass of glass in the constricted part becomes so thick as to be difficult to handle when hot, and likely to crack on cooling. Larger tubes are therefore constricted by heating in a narrow flame, with constant rotation, and when soft, alternately gently pulling the ends apart and pushing them together, each motion being so regulated that the diameter of a short section of the tube is gradually reduced, while the thickness of the wall of the reduced portion remains the same as that of the rest of the tube, or increases only slightly. This pulling and pushing of the glass takes place *in the flame*, while the rotation is being continued regularly. The result may appear as indicated in c, Fig. 1. The strength of the work depends upon the thickness of the walls of the constricted portion, which should never be less than that in the main tube, and usually a little greater. This operation is most successful with tubing having a relatively thin wall.

Flanging a Tube.—This operation produces the characteristic flange seen on test-tubes, necks of flasks, etc., the object being twofold: to finish the end neatly and to strengthen it so that a cork may be inserted without breaking it. This flanging may be done in several ways. In any case the first operation is to cut the tube to a square end, and then heat this end so that the extreme sixteenth or eighth of an inch of it is soft and begins to shrink. The tube is of course rotated during this heat-

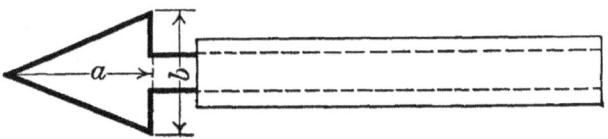

FIG. 2.—Flanging tool.

ing, which should take place in a flame of slightly greater diameter than the tube, if possible. The flange is now produced by expanding this softened part with some suitable tool. A cone of charcoal has been recommended for this purpose, and works fairly well, if made so its height is about equal to the diameter of its base. The tube is rotated and the cone, held in the other hand, is pressed into the open end until the flange is formed. A pyramid with eight or ten sides would probably be better than the cone.

A better flanging tool is made from a triangular piece of copper or brass, about 1/16 inch thick, and mounted in a suitable handle. Such a tool is shown in Fig. 2, being cut from a sheet of copper and provided with a handle made by wrapping asbestos paper moistened with sodium silicate solution about the shank of the tool. It is well to have several sizes and shapes of these tools, for different sizes of tubing. The two sizes most used will be those having about the following dimensions: (1) $a=2$ inches, $b=1$ inch; (2) $a=1$ inch, $b=1$ inch. When the end of the tube is softened, the tool is inserted

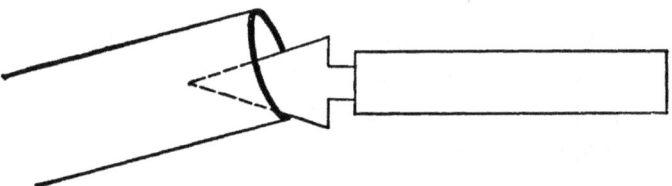

Fig. 3.—Flanging a tube with flanging tool.

at an angle, as indicated in Fig. 3, and pressed against the soft part, while the tube is quickly rotated about its axis. If the flange is insufficient the operation may be repeated. The tool should always be warmed in the flame before use, and occasionally greased by touching it to a piece of wax or paraffin. After the flange is complete, the end must be heated again to the softening temperature and cooled slowly, to prevent it from cracking.

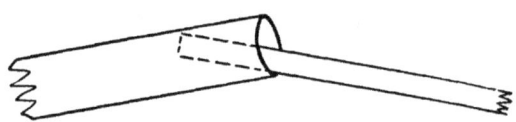

Fig. 4.—Flanging a tube with carbon rod or wire.

Some glass-blowers use a small carbon rod, about 3/16 inch in diameter, as a flanging tool for tubes larger than about 3/8 inch diameter, and a small iron wire or similar piece of metal for smaller tubes. In this case the tube is heated as above described, and the rod or wire inserted in the end at an angle and pressed against the softened part, as indicated in Fig. 4, while the tube is rotated about its axis. For large heavy tubes a larger carbon would be used.

Rotation of the Tube.—This is the fundamental manipulation in glass-blowing, and upon it more than all else depends the uniformity and finish of the work, and often the possibility of accomplishing the work at all. Directions for it will be given on the assumption that the reader is right-handed; if otherwise, the position of the hands is of course reversed. The object of rotation is to insure even heating of the whole circumference of the tube at the point of attack, to equalize the effect of gravity on the hot glass and prevent it from falling out of shape when soft, and to keep the parts of the tube on each side of the heated portion in the same straight line.

In rotating the tube, both hands must be used, so that the two ends may revolve at the same rate and the glass in the hot part not be twisted. The rotation is performed by the thumb and first finger of each hand, the other fingers serving to support the tube. As it is almost always necessary to follow rotating and heating a tube by blowing it, the hands should be so placed that it will be easy to bring the right-hand end up to the mouth without shifting the hold on the glass. For this reason the lefs hand grasps the glass with the palm down, and the right hand with the palm turned toward the left. If there it any choice, the longer and heavier part of the tube is usually given to the left hand, and it is planned to blow into the shorter end. This is because it is easier to support the tube with the hand which has the palm down. This support is accomplished by bending the hand at the wrist so that it points slightly downward, and then curling the second, third and little fingers in under the tube, which is held between them and the palm. This support should be loose enough so that the thumb and first finger can easily cause the tube to rotate regularly on its axis, but firm enough to carry all the weight of the tube, leaving the thumb and first finger nothing to do but rotate it. The hand must be so turned, and the other fingers so bent, that the thumb and first finger stretch out nearly to their full length to grasp the tube comfortably.

The right hand is held with the palm toward the left, the fingers except the first slightly bent, and the tube held between the first finger and the thumb while it rests on the second finger and that portion of the hand between the base of the first finger and the thumb. Rotation of the tube is accomplished by rolling it between the thumbs and first fingers: the rotation being continued in the same direction regularly, and not reversed. It is better to roll slowly and evenly, with a series of light touches, each of which moves the tube a little, than to attempt to turn the tube a half a revolution or so with each motion of the hands. The hands must be held steady, and the tube must be under good control at all times, so that both ends may be rotated at the same angular velocity, even though they may be of different diameters, and the tube be neither drawn apart nor pushed together unless such a motion is expressly desired, as it sometimes is. The hot part of the glass must be constantly watched to see that it is uniformly rotated and not twisted, nor pulled out or pushed together more than is desired. Care must also be taken to keep the parts of the tube in the same straight line, or as near it as possible, during the heating and all other manipulations.

When flanging a tube, it is held and rotated with the left hand as above described, while the right hand holds the flanging tool.

When part of the end of a tube must be heated, as in Exercise 6, and rotation must be very carefully performed and continued during the blowing, both hands are used.

The right hand is held as above described, and the left hand close to it and either as above described or else with the palm toward the right, grasping the tube in the same way as the right hand does. This puts both hands in a position where the tube may be blown and rotated uniformly while its axis is kept horizontal.

Smoothness and exactness are the two things for which the beginner must constantly strive in glass-blowing, and they are only attained by a careful attention to the details of manipulation, with a steady hand and watchful eye. Every move must count, and the exercise must be finished with a minimum of reheating and retouching, for the best results.

CHAPTER III

Elementary Exercises

EXERCISE NO. 1

Joining Two Pieces of Tubing, End to End—First Method

This exercise is most easily learned on tubing with an exterior diameter of 1/4 inch, or a little less, having moderately heavy walls. A piece of such tubing is heated before

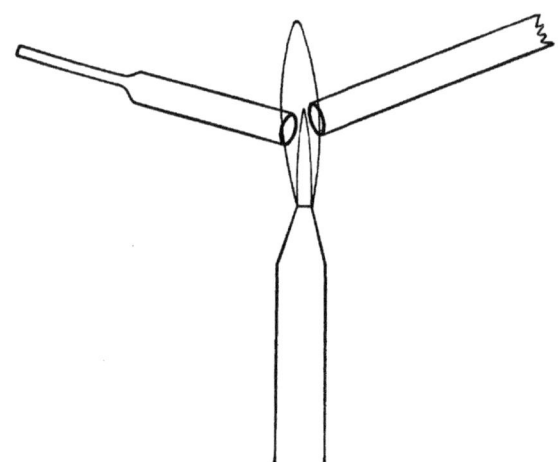

Fig. 5.—Softening ends of two pieces of tubing.

the blow-pipe at a point ten or twelve inches from the end, and there drawn out to a capillary as previously described (page 9). The capillary is sealed off about two inches from the main tube, and the latter is cut near the middle. Care should be taken to get square ends where the cut is made (page 7). The flame is now so regulated that it is a little broader than the diameter of the tube, the sealed half of the tube taken in the left hand and the other half in the right. The open end of the sealed part and one of the ends of the other part are now held in opposite sides of the flame, inclined at a slight angle to one another as indicated in Fig. 5, and rotated and heated until the surfaces of both ends are just softened. The two ends are then carefully and

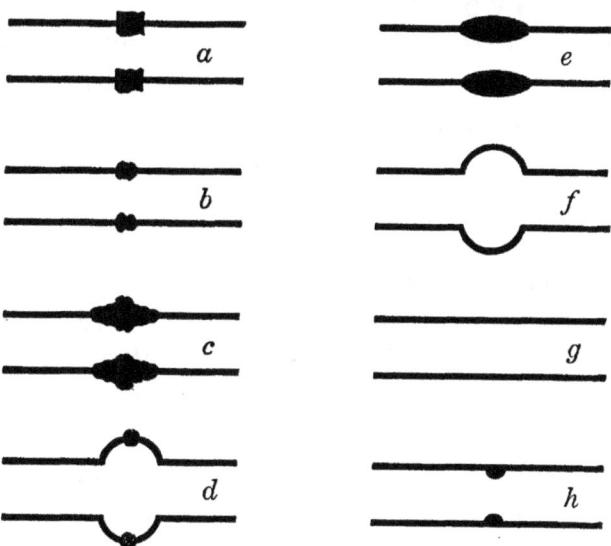

FIG. 6.—Joining two pieces of tubing end to end—first method.

quickly brought together (*a*, Fig. 6), removed from the flame and pulled apart a little, to reduce the lump formed at the joint as much as possible, as indicated in *b*. The joint is then tested by blowing into the open end of the tube to see if it is tight. If so, the flame is reduced to half or less than half of its former size, and the joint heated in it, holding the tube and continually rotating it as directed in the last chapter (page 13).

As the tube softens and tends to shrink, the two ends are pressed together a little and the walls allowed to thicken slightly, as in *c*. It is then quickly removed from the flame and gently blown as indicated in *d*, continuing the rotation of the tube during the blowing, and at the same time pressing the ends of the tube together a little so as to make a *short* thick-walled bulb. The joint is then returned to the flame and reheated, rotating as before, shrinking to about the shape of *e*. When this stage is reached, the glass should be very hot and fluid, and the mass of hot glass thick enough to remain at its working temperature for about five seconds after removal from the flame. The glass is now reblown as indicated in *f*, to form a bulb having walls of practically the same thickness as the original tube. As soon as the bulb is blown, the tube is removed from the mouth, held horizontally in front of the worker, and gently drawn out to form one continuous tube, as indicated in *g*. During both the blowing and drawing of this bulb the rotation must be continued, and both blowing and drawing must be carefully regulated so that the resulting tube may have the same internal and external diameter at the joint as elsewhere.

Discussion.—In making the original joint (*a*, Fig. 6), care should be taken that the lump formed is as small as possible so that it may be entirely removed during the subsequent operations. For this reason, only the very tip ends of the two pieces of tubing are held in the flame, and the softening should not extend more than 1/16 inch down the tube. As soon as the ends are sufficiently soft to stick together, they are made to do so. The first drawing of the tube (*b*) should take place immediately, and reduce the lump as much as possible without making the adjacent walls of the tube thin. The whole purpose of the rest of the manipulation is to absorb or "iron out" the lump at the joint. For this reason, care is taken that this lump is always in the center of the flame while the joint is being heated, and a small flame is used so that little of the main tube may be softened. During the first shrinking of the joint (c) the walls next the lump, being thinner than it is, reach the softening temperature first and are thickened by the slight pushing together of the ends, so that they taper from the lump to the unchanged wall. Upon blowing this joint, these thickened walls blow out with the lump, but as they are thinnest next the unchanged tube, they stiffen there first. Then as the thicker parts are still hot, these blow out more, and with the lump make a more or less uniform wall. By this first operation most of the lump will have been removed, provided it was not too large at first, and the tube was hot enough when it was blown. Beginners almost invariably have the glass too cool here, and find difficulty in blowing out a satisfactory bulb. Under such circumstances the lump will be scarcely affected by the operation.

During the shrinking of this bulb, the thinner parts of course are the first to reach the softening point, and thus contract more than the thick parts, so that practically all of the lump can be absorbed, and a uniformly thickened part of the tube left as in e. When this is just accomplished, the second bulb must be blown during one or two seconds, and the tube then drawn out as described, so as to change the bulb to a tube. The drawing must proceed with care: portions nearest the unchanged tubes are the first to reach the proper diameter, and must be given time to just set at that point before the center of the bulb is finally drawn into shape. The drawing is perhaps best done intermittently in a series of quick pulls, each drawing the tube perhaps 1/16 inch, and each taking place as the thumbs and first fingers grasp the tube for a new turn in the rotation. If the tube is not rotated during the blowing, the bulbs will be lop-sided and it will be impossible to get a joint of uniform wall-thickness;

if rotation is omitted during the drawing, the tube will almost invariably be quite crooked.

If the lump still shows distinctly after the operations described, the cross-section of the tube will be as in h, and the tube will be likely to break if ever reheated at this point after it becomes cold. The operations d, e, f, and g may be repeated upon it, and it may be possible to get it to come out all right.

Care must be taken not to blow the bulbs d and f too thin as they then become very difficult to handle, and the joint is usually spoiled. The wall-thickness of these bulbs must never be much less than that of the original tube. If the joint as completed has thinner walls than the rest of the tube, it will be more easily broken. It should be remembered that the length of the finished tube must be exactly the same as that of the original piece, if the walls of the joint are to be of their original thickness. Therefore the pushing together during the two operations c and d must shorten the tube just as much as the final drawing (f to g) lengthens it.

The interval between the removal of the work from the flame and the beginning of the blowing must be made as short as possible, or else the portions next the main parts of the tube will set before they can be blown out, and cause irregular shrunken areas.

EXERCISE NO. 2

Joining Two Tubes End to End—Second Method

The method described in Exercise No. 1 is very satisfactory for joining short lengths of straight tubing, but becomes inconvenient or impossible when the pieces are long or bent, on account of the difficulty in uniformly rotating such work. In such cases, this second method is used. It does not usually give as smooth and pretty a joint as the first method, and takes a little longer.

The joint is begun exactly as in the first method, and the manipulation is the same until after the preliminary tight joint (b, Fig. 6) is made. The flame is reduced as usual, but instead of rotating the tube in the flame, only one part of the circumference is heated, and this is allowed to shrink thoroughly before blowing. It is then blown gently so that it becomes a slight swelling on the tube, and the operation repeated on an adjoining part of the joint. Three or four repetitions of the operation will usually cover the whole circumference of the joint, in a small tube, the result being a swelling roughly similar to the first thick bulb in the first method (d, Fig. 6). If all the lumps of the original joint have not been removed by this operation, it may now be repeated upon such parts as may require it. The thickness of the wall in the bulb should be about the same as that in the original tube. The whole of the expanded joint is now heated as uniformly as may be until soft enough so that it begins to shrink a little, and the swelling is gently drawn down to the same diameter as the main tube, as in the first case. Any irregularities in the finished joint may be corrected by local reheating, shrinking or blowing as required.

Discussion.—In using this method, especially with larger sizes of tubing, it is very important to keep the whole circumference of the joint hot enough during the operation so that it does not crack apart at the part which has not yet been worked. For that reason the first heating, shrinking and blowing should be performed as quickly as possible, leaving the resulting irregularities to be corrected later, rather than attempting to reblow the same part of the joint several times in succession until it is satisfactory. Care must be taken in this as in the first method that the blowing follows immediately upon the completion of the shrinking and removal of the object from the flame: delay in blowing will cause shrunken places where the joint meets the original tubes, on account of the cooling and setting of the glass before it was blown. Most beginners err in being afraid to shrink the part of the joint enough before blowing it. On small tubing, the shrinkage may often extend so far that the inner surface of the shrunken part reaches the center of the tube. Insufficient shrinking results in failure to remove the lump formed at the original joint. It is often of advantage, after blowing out part of the joint, to allow that part a few seconds to set before going on with the rest, keeping the whole joint warm meanwhile in or near the smoky flame. This helps to prevent the twisting of the joint, or other distortion incident to the handling of a piece of work of awkward shape.

In making a joint on a very long or heavy piece by this method, it is often advantageous to attach a piece of rubber tubing to the open end, hold the other end of this tubing in the mouth during the process, and blow through it, rather than attempt to bring the end of the glass up to the mouth. This enables one to keep closer watch on the joint, and avoid drawing it out or distorting it in handling. On the other hand, the rubber tube is an inconvenience on account of its weight and the consequent pull on the end of the apparatus, and makes rotation difficult.

EXERCISE NO. 3

THE "TEE" TUBE

The operations involved are two: the blowing of a short side tube on a piece of tubing, and sealing another piece of tubing on this, by what is essentially the second method as just described.

The two pieces of tubing to be used each have one end cut square and the other sealed in the usual manner. The longer of the two is now heated at the point at which the joint is to be made, until it begins to color the flame. A small flame is used, and the tube rotated until the flame begins to be colored, when the rotation is stopped, and only one spot heated until a spot the diameter of the tube to be sealed on has become red hot and begun to shrink. This is now gently blown out into a small bulb, as in *a*, Fig. 7, and it will be noted that this bulb will have walls tapering from the thick walls of the tube to a very thin wall at the top. The sides of this bulb, below the dotted line, are to form the small side tube to which the main side tube is to be sealed. The top of the bulb is now softened by directing a small flame directly upon it, and as soon as it shrinks to the level indicated by the dotted line, it is removed from the flame and quickly blown out to form a thin bulb, as indicated in *b*, Fig. 7. This will usu-

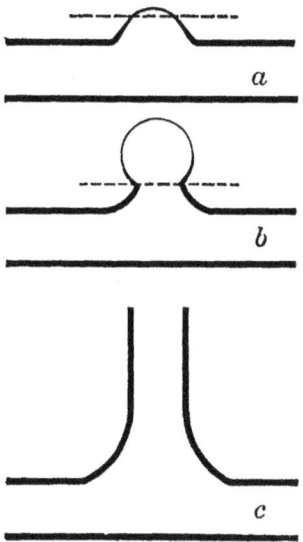

Fig. 7.—The "tee" tube.

ally be so very thin that a stroke of the file or glass-knife will break it off at the dotted line, leaving the side tube, to which the short piece of tubing is now sealed according to the second method (Exercise No 2). In doing this, care is taken to direct the flame partly on the main tube in the two crotches, so that both tubes blow out a little and give space for the gases to turn in, as indicated in *c*, Fig. 7, and at the same time increase the mechanical strength of the job. On the other hand, care is taken not to deform the main tube, and not to produce such a bulge or bulb at the joint as will prevent the finished tube from lying flat on a table.

Discussion.—Most beginners tend to err in the first steps of this operation, by blowing too hard and too long when blowing out the little bulb. The result is a large, very thin bulb, which breaks off in such a way as to leave a hole in the main tube, occupying nearly half the circumference of the tube at that point, instead of the neat side tube which they should have. It is not difficult to seal a tube on this side tube, but it is very difficult to seal a tube into a hole in another tube. Care should be taken here, as in the two previous exercises, that the lump obtained at the joint when the two tubes are put together is made as small as possible, and reduced if possible by gently drawing on the side tube as soon as the tubes have actually joined. It is much easier to prevent the formation of a lump at the joint than it is to remove the lump after it is formed. The remarks previously made about blowing quickly after removing the work from the flame apply here with especial force. A "tee" tube, from its very nature, is exposed to a good many strains, so care must be taken that the walls of the joint are of uniform thickness with the rest of the tube.

The beginner will find it easiest to make this tube out of two pieces of the same tube, about 1/4 inch in diameter. Larger or smaller tubing is usually more difficult. If tubing much more than 1/4 inch is used, the whole joint, including part of the main tube, must be heated nearly to the softening point at the close of the operation, and well annealed; as described in Chapter I (page 3) or it will be almost certain to crack. In the larger sizes of tube it will be necessary to heat the whole circumference of the main tube frequently during the operation, to prevent it from cracking.

In sealing a small tube on the side of a large one, it is

usually advisable, after warming the spot where the joint is to be made, to attach a small drop of glass to the tube at that point, and direct the flame upon that, thus supplying at the same time both a definite point to be heated and an extra supply of glass for the little side tube which is desired. In this way it is also easier to blow out a side tube with a sufficiently small diameter. If the diameter of this tube should be much greater than that of the small tube, the latter may be enlarged with a carbon or a flanging tool.

EXERCISE NO. 4

To Join Two Tubes of Different Diameters

In this case the first method (Exercise No. 1) is to be used whenever possible, as it gives a much smoother joint than the second method. The directions given will describe the adaptation of this method to the problem: if the second method must be used on account of awkward shape, etc., of the work, the modifications required will be obvious to any one who has learned to make the joint by the first method.

After sealing or corking one end of the larger tube, the other end is drawn out to form a tail as described on page 9, taking care to have the tube uniformly heated, and to draw the tail rapidly enough so that the cone is short, as indicated in a, Fig. 8. The tube is now rotated, a small flame directed against the cone at right angles to an element of it, and it is allowed to shrink a little, as indicated in b, Fig. 8, so that its walls will thicken. When the tail is cut off, at the dotted line, the diameter of the opening and the thickness of the walls at that point should correspond with the dimensions of the tube to be sealed on. As the glass is hot, the scratch for cutting it must be made with a file (moisten the edge!), and it often will not break square across. Before proceeding to seal on the small tube, any large projections on the cut end are best removed, by warming the cut surface a little, directing the small flame upon each projection in turn and touching it with a warm scrap of glass. It will adhere to this and may then be removed by rotating this scrap a little so as to wind up the projection on it, and then drawing it off, while the flame is still playing on the spot. This must be done rapidly and care taken not to soften the main part of the cone.

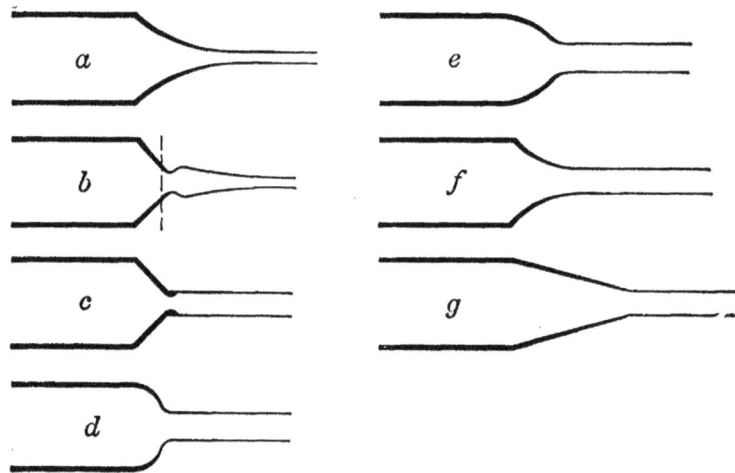

FIG. 8.—Joining two tubes of different diameters.

The large tube is now taken in the left hand, the small one in the right, the ends heated and joined in the usual manner, taking care not to get any larger lump at the joint than necessary. A small flame is now directed on the cone at right angles to its elements as before, and the tube rotated so as to heat the whole circumference. The flame should be just large enough to heat the whole of the cone. As the latter shrinks, the lump at the joint is brought into the edge of the flame, and it and a very little of the small tube allowed to shrink with the cone.

When well shrunk and heated to blowing temperature the joint is removed from the flame and blown gently with careful rotation, pushing the tubes together a little when the blowing is about finished, so that the cone becomes a short thick half-bulb, as shown in d, Fig. 8. This corresponds to the first thick bulb in the first method (d, Fig. 6), and is treated similarly. It is again heated and shrunk, taking care not to involve either the large tube or the small one in the shrinking, blown quickly to about the same shape as before, (d, Fig. 8), and then gently drawn out into a smooth cone (e), exactly as in the first exercise. Care should be taken not to draw too rapidly or too far, as then the resulting cone (f) is weaker than it should be, and does not look well.

Discussion.—The beginner will find that this operation is best learned on two tubes which are not too nearly of the same diameter. A tube about 5/8 inch in diameter and one a little less than 1/4 inch will be suitable. Both should have moderately heavy walls (1/16 inch or a trifle over for the large tube, and a trifle less for the small one) but the large tube should not be too heavy or else it will be hard to prevent melting down too much of the small tube, and getting this drawn out too thin during the process. One of the troublesome features of this exercise is the difficulty of rotating two tubes of different diameters with the same angular velocity, so as not to twist the joint. Another difficulty is found in getting the cone uniformly heated to blowing temperature without overheating and overshrinking the small tube. The reason for this is obviously the much greater circumference of the cone, especially at its large end, so that relatively much less of it is being heated at any time. The beginner is also inclined to start with too long a cone, or else heat so much of the large tube that part of its glass is included in the cone, with the result that in order to get the right wall-thickness the cone must be made too long (*g*, Fig. 8). This does not look well, and usually will be irregular in shape.

EXERCISE NO. 5

Tube for Condensing Sulphur Dioxide

This is useful as a test of mastery of the preceding exercise. A piece of 3/16 or 7/32 inch tubing is joined to each end of a piece of tubing 5/8 by about 5 inches, and two constrictions made in the large tube, by the method described on page 10. The small tubes are then bent

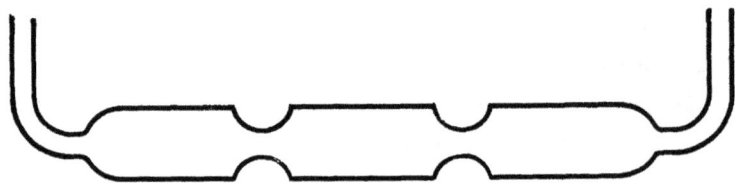

Fig. 9.—Tube for condensing sulphur dioxide.

in the same plane, as shown, and their ends fire-polished (Fig. 9)

EXERCISE NO. 6

Bulb at the End of a Tube

For this exercise tubing of 1/4 inch diameter and moderately strong walls is selected. A tail is drawn out on one end of the tube, and a piece of tubing about nine or ten inches long is cut off. The tail should be carefully drawn in the axis of the tube, and in the same straight line with it, as it is to be used as a handle in assembling the glass for the bulb. This tail must be long enough so that it can be conveniently held in the left hand, as described on page 13, and rotated about the same axis as the main tube. Holding the main tube in the right hand and the tail in the left, the tube is rotated in a large flame so that a piece of it, beginning where the tail stops and extending about an inch to the right, may be uniformly heated to the highest temperature at which it can be kept in shape. As soon as this temperature is reached, the tube is removed from the flame, continuing the rotation and taking care not to draw out the heated part, and gently blown. The rotation is carefully continued during the blowing, holding the tube in approximately a horizontal position. As soon as the tube has expanded a little the tail is pushed gently toward the main tube, continuing the gentle blowing. If this is properly done, the heated piece of tube will become a short bulb of about double its original diameter, and about the same wall thickness as the original tube. It will have somewhat the appearance of a, Fig. 10, when properly manipulated.

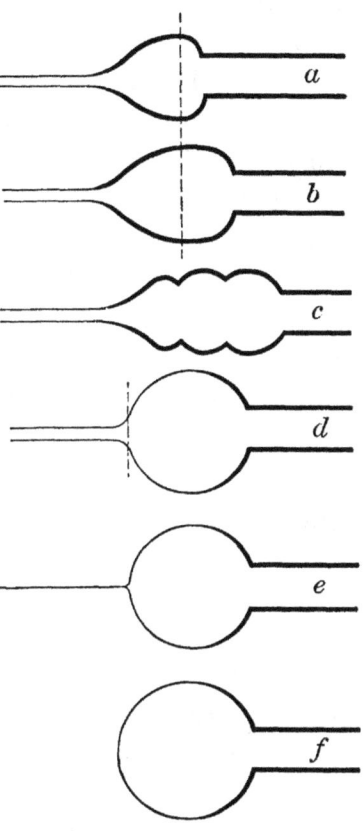

FIG. 10 —Blowing a bulb on the end of a tube.

The tube is now reheated as before, taking care this time that the heating extends over all that part of the bulb to the right of the dotted line in the figure, as well as part of the main tube adjoining. If this heating has been properly placed, when the operation of blowing and pushing together is repeated the result will be to lengthen the bulb into a uniform cylinder, as shown in b, Fig. 10. Otherwise the result will be a series of bulbs, as in e,

Fig. 10, separated by thickened ridges which will be almost impossible of removal later and will disfigure the final bulb. This operation of heating, blowing and pushing together is repeated several times, until the cylinder becomes as long as can be conveniently handled (about 1 1/4 inches to 1 1/2 inches). If more glass is needed than is then contained in the cylinder, the latter may now be heated as a whole, and blown and pushed gently into a shorter cylinder of a slightly greater diameter, and more glass then added as before.

When enough glass has been collected for the bulb, it is all well heated and blown gently a couple of times, pushing the mass together as required, until a thick bulb like *d*, Fig. 10, is obtained. The tail must now be removed at the point indicated by the dotted line. To do this, a very fine flame is directed on the point where the tail joins the bulb, and the tube well rotated as the glass softens at that point. When sufficiently soft, the work is raised a little, so that the flame instead of striking the glass squarely at the point indicated passes below and tangential to it. The tail is now drawn off slowly, continuing the rotation, raising the work just out of the flame whenever the thread of glass drawn off becomes too thin, and lowering it again to the point where the flame just touches it when the glass stiffens a little. By this means the tail may be drawn off without leaving an appreciable lump behind, as indicated in *e* and *f*, Fig. 10. When as much of the extra glass has been removed as is practicable, the flame is brought to play squarely upon the little lump left, the last of the tail removed, and the lump heated and gently blown to a small excrescence on the main bulb. The whole end of the latter is now heated until it begins to shrink a little, and gently blown to make it uniform in thickness. The whole bulb is then heated in a flame of the proper size, so that it all may shrink to about two-thirds of its diameter. The flame must be very carefully chosen and directed, so as to shrink all the bulb, right up to the main tube, but not soften the latter. As soon as this stage is reached, the bulb is removed from the flame, continuing the even rotation, and blown to the desired size, preferably by a series of gentle puffs following one another at very short intervals. During the blowing, the main tube is held in a horizontal position, and any tendency of the bulb to fall out of line is corrected by the rotation. If the shape of the bulb or its size are not satisfactory, it may be shrunk again and reblown. Such shrinking should begin in a large yellow flame, with just enough air to give it direction. The amount of air may be gradually increased as the bulb shrinks and the walls become thick enough to bear it without collapsing. If the bulb starts to collapse at any time, it must be immediately blown enough to regain its convex surface, before the shrinking proceeds further.

Discussion.—In collecting the glass for the bulb, enough must be gathered to give the walls the desired strength. Since the area of a sphere is proportional to the cube of its diameter, it is evident that doubling the size of a bulb diminishes the thickness of its walls to a very large extent. The limit of diameter for a strong bulb on ordinary 1/4-inch tubing, collecting the glass as above, is about 1 1/2 inches, and the beginner will do well not to blow his bulbs more than an inch in diameter.

The collection of the glass is one of the most important parts of the process. If the mass of glass be twisted, furrowed or ridged, or lopsided, it is very difficult to get a good, even, spherical bulb, no matter how many times it is shrunk and blown. The greatest care should therefore be taken to get a uniform cylinder, on the same axis as the main tube; and to this end the rotation of the tube must be carried on very evenly. For method of holding the tube, see page 14.

If a very large bulb is required, it will often be economical to seal on the end of the tube a short piece of a large tube, provided with the proper tail, and use the glass in the large tube for the bulb instead of attempting to collect it from the small tube. In this case part of the small tube will usually be included in the bulb, so that the joint comes in the latter, and not where it joins the tube. As the amount of glass carried on the end of the tube increases in weight and size the difficulties of heating it uniformly, keeping it in the proper position and handling it increase rapidly.

In collecting glass, it is usually best not to leave the part of the cylinder next the tube with too thick walls. This is always the coolest part during the preparation for blowing the bulb, consequently it does not get blown out, and causes an ugly thickened appearance on that end of the bulb.

If the bulb grows too long or pear-shaped, it may be easily shortened by heating to the blowing temperature, and then blowing gently with the main tube in a vertical position, and the bulb at the top of it. Gravity will then shorten the bulb nicely.

The finished bulb should be a nearly perfect sphere, with the axis of the tube passing through its center, and the portion of the tube adjoining the bulb must not be distorted, twisted, or blown out. In order to prevent the distortion of the tube, care must be taken that it is never heated quite to its softening point during the process.

EXERCISE NO. 7

BLOWING A BULB IN A TUBE

The tube is selected and one end closed as in the previous exercise, but it should be cut a little longer, say about twelve inches. Beginning at a point about four inches from the closed end, glass is collected and blown into a thick-walled bulb, exactly as in the previous exercise. Greater care must be taken, however, that the cylinder collected and this thick bulb are of uniform thickness and set squarely in the axis of the tube. Instead of removing the tail, the bulb must be blown in this case with both pieces of tubing attached, and care must be taken that they "line up" properly, *i.e.*, are in the same straight line, and that this line passes as near as may be through the center of the bulb. The tube is held in approximately horizontal position during the blowing of the bulb, as in the previous case, and especial care taken with the rotation. Both pieces of tube must of course be rotated at the same rate, and their softened ends must be kept at exactly the proper distance from each other, so that the bulb may be spherical and not elongated. If the blowing of the bulb be quickly and accurately done, it may usually be completed before the glass is quite set, and the alignment of the two tubes may then be rectified while looking straight through the bore of the tube.

Discussion.—The two points of greatest importance are the collection of the glass, and the uniform rotation of the tube. A larger tube may be sealed in the middle of a small one when a large amount of glass is necessary. The piece of tubing used for the exercise must be long enough so that the fingers may be kept on a cool part of the glass without getting uncomfortably near the ends of the tube. It should not be any longer than necessary, however, as the extra weight and length make the manipulation of the hot glass more difficult.

When a string of bulbs are required on the same tube, a piece of glass 18 inches long may be used at the start, and the first bulb made near the closed end, as described. Each succeeding bulb will then be in plain view during the blowing, and when the open end becomes too short for comfort, it may be dried out, cut off, and another piece joined to it, starting as in the first method (Exercise No. 1), but instead of drawing out the thick bulb to a tube, it is made part of the glass collected for the next bulb. If the string of bulbs becomes awkward to handle on account of its length and weight, it may be made in several parts and these later sealed together by the second method, preferably blowing through a rubber tube attached to the open end, as described on page 22.

Very neat small bulbs may be made on tubing of a diameter of 3/16 inch or a little less, but the beginner is advised to start with tubing of about 1/4 inch diameter. The use of tubing with too thick walls usually produces bulbs which are thick-walled at the point where they leave the tube, but inclined to be too thin at the point of maximum diameter (perpendicular to the axis of the tube) where most of the strain comes and strength is particularly needed.

CHAPTER IV

Advanced Exercises

EXERCISE NO. 8

Sealing a Tube Through Another Tube

First Method—Making a Gas-washing Tube

This first method can be used whenever one can work through an open end opposite to the end of the tube where the joint is to be made. To illustrate it, take a piece of rather thin-walled tubing, about 3/4 inch in diameter, and some pieces of rather strong tubing a little less than 1/4 inch in diameter. Draw off the large tube in a short cone, then draw off the tail as in the making of the bulb on the end of the tube, blow out the little lump slightly, shrink the whole cone a little and blow gently to form a rounded end like that on a test-tube, with walls about the thickness of those of the rest of the tube. Cut this tube to a suitable length, say about six inches, and provide two corks which will fit the open end of it. Now cut a piece of the small tubing of the proper length to form the piece which is to be inside the large tube. For practice purposes, this piece should be about an inch shorter than the large tube. Flange one end of this tube a little, and anneal the flange well in the smoky flame. Bore one of the corks so that a piece of the small tubing will fit it, and cut a couple of notches in the side of this cork so that air can pass between it and the glass. Pass a short piece of the small tubing through this cork, and attach the flanged piece of small tube to this by means of a short piece of rubber tubing, so that when the whole is inserted in the large tube it is arranged as in *a*, Fig. 11. The piece of glass tubing projecting out through the cork is now cut off so as to leave an end about 1/2 inch long when the cork is firmly seated and the inner tube pushed into contact with the center of the end of the large tube, as

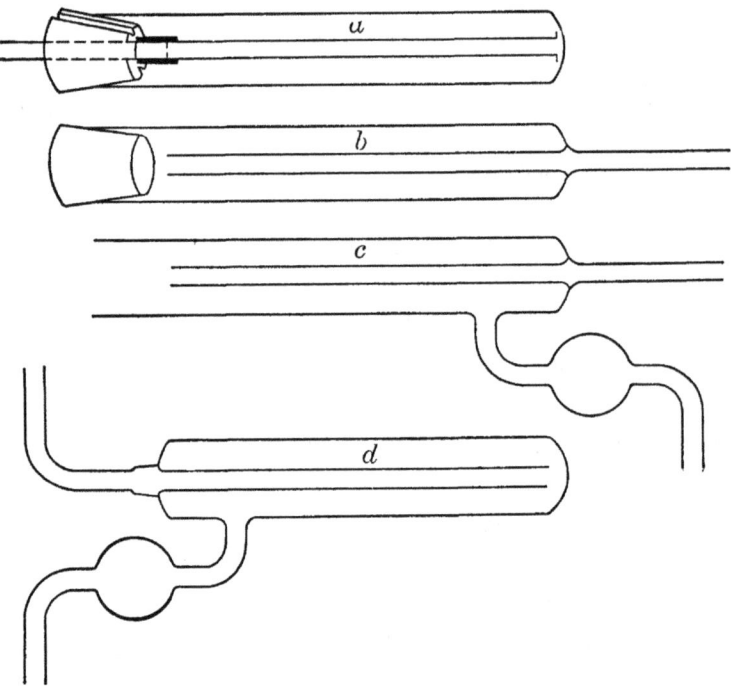

Fig. 11.—Gas-washing tube.

shown in the drawing. Care should be taken that the little rubber tube which joins the two pieces is arranged as in the figure; *i.e.*, most of it on the piece of tubing which passes through the cork, and very little on the other piece, so that when the cork is removed after the small tube has been sealed through the large one, the rubber tube may easily come with it. Select a short piece of the small tubing of suitable length for the piece which is to be on the outside of the large tube as a continuation of the piece inside, and another piece for the delivery tube. A small bulb may be blown in the latter at a point about 2 1/2 inches from the closed end, and the open end cut off about 1 1/2 inches from the bulb. A cork or cork-boring of suitable size to stopper the small tube is prepared, and laid ready with the other (unbored) cork for the large tube.

When everything is in readiness, the rounded end of the large tube is slowly heated until it softens and joins firmly to the small tube inside. After it has shrunk down well, it is blown out to its original size, placing the whole end of the large tube, cork and all, in the mouth. Now with a fine-pointed flame the glass covering the end of the small tube is heated to the softening temperature, and then is blown out to an excrescence by blowing on the end of the small tube which passes through the cork. The end of this excrescence is heated and blown off in the usual way, so as to leave the small tube sealed on the inside of the large one and opening through it into this short tube which has been blown out. The end of the small tube which passes through the cork is now closed with the cork prepared for it, and the short outer tube is joined to the tube that has just been blown out, so that the joint appears like *b*, Fig. 11. Use the first method (Exercise No. 1) for this joint. Reheat the whole of the end of the tube nearly to the softening temperature, anneal it a little, and allow to cool a few seconds until well set. Now remove the cork, short glass tube and rubber tube from the open end of the large tube and insert the solid cork in their place. Warm the joint and the whole of that end of the tube again carefully up to about the softening point, then seal on the side tube for the delivery of the gas in the usual way, taking care that the whole of the end and the joint are kept warm meanwhile. When thoroughly sealed, the delivery tube is bent up parallel to the tube through which the gas enters, and then out at right angles to it, as shown in c. The whole of the end of the tube is now cautiously reheated and then cooled slowly to anneal it.

The cork may now be removed from the open end of the large tube, this end heated in a large flame, caught together with a scrap of glass tubing and drawn off into a cone so that the base of the cone is about opposite the end of the inner tube. The lump of glass is drawn off the point of this cone and it is reblown to form a rounded end, as previously described.

After this cools, the tube through which the gas enters may be heated at the proper point and bent at right angles to form the finished apparatus as shown in d. The ends of the small tube are cut off square and fire-polished.

Discussion.—After the joint has once been made, great care must be taken that it is kept hot during all the subsequent manipulations, and if it becomes somewhat cool at any time it must be reheated very slowly. It is obvious that the rate of heating and cooling of the inner tube will be slower than that of the outer tube, and this will readily produce stresses which tend to crack the tube at the joint. The amount of heating and cooling which such a joint will stand depends upon its form. The beginner should examine such a joint on regular factory-made apparatus, and note the uniformity of wall-thickness and the "clean-cut" appearance of the joint, as a model for his imitation. A ragged joint, where the line of joining of the inner and outer tubes wavers instead of going squarely around the tube, is almost sure to crack during the cooling and heating unless extra precautions are taken with it. The presence of a small lump of glass at any point on the joint affords an excellent starting place for a crack, as do also the points on a ragged joint where the inner tube comes farther down on the outer tube than at other points.

In order to insure a joint which is square and not ragged, it is essential that the angle between the inner and outer tubes at the joint be very nearly a right angle. For this reason the two tubes should not be of too near the same size, or if this cannot be avoided, a small bulb should be blown on the end where the joint is to be made. If this bulb be made with the same wall-thickness as the rest of the tube, and somewhat pear-shaped, it may be drawn out to the same size as the rest of the tube, if necessary, after the joint has been made.

This method is used wherever possible in preference to the second method (Exercise No. 9), as it is easier to get a good joint with it. It may also be used where it is desired to seal the tube through the side of a tube, or for a tube sealed through the wall of a bulb, as in a Geissler potash bulb or similar apparatus. Where there is not space to join the inner tube to the blowing tube by a rubber tube, this joint may be made with a small piece of gummed paper, which can readily be broken when desired.

EXERCISE NO. 9

SEALING A TUBE THROUGH ANOTHER TUBE

Second Method—Making a Suction Pump

Select a piece of tubing 3/8 to 1/2 inch in diameter, with walls about 1/16 inch or a little less in thickness, heat a place about 4 inches from one end and draw it out so that when cut off at the proper point it will look like *a*, Fig. 12; the open end of the drawn out part being small enough to slip inside another piece of the original tube. A small thick-walled bulb is now blown as indicated by the dotted lines, and annealed. A piece of the original tubing is now prepared, 7 or 8 inches long, with one end cut square off and the other closed. A piece of 1/4-in tubing about 2 inches long, and drawn out at one end to a tail several inches long is also prepared, to form the inlet tube for the air. Another piece of the 3/8-inch tube is prepared, about 4 inches long, and provided with a tail drawn out as indicated in b, so that when cut off at about 2 1/2 or 3 inches from the main tube its inner diameter may be slightly less than that of the narrowest point of the tube a. A small thick-walled bulb is blown at the point indicated by the dotted lines, and

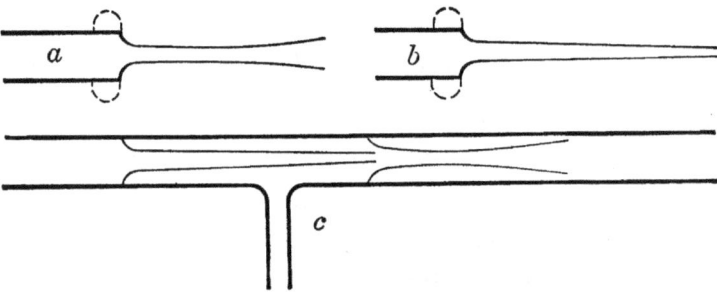

Fig. 12.—Suction pump.

annealed. Care must be taken in drawing the capillary and blowing the bulb in both a and b that the capillary tubes are in the axis of the main tube, and in the same straight line with it.

The open end of the 8-inch piece of tube and the bulb of the piece a are now warmed together, the end of the tube only moderately and the bulb to about its softening temperature. The tube a is now inserted in the open end of the large tube, and the bulb softened with a suitable flame and pressed into good contact with the tube. It is then reheated, including the joint, blown a little and pulled out to form a straight tube in line with the main tube. By warming the joint a little, and proper rotation, the capillary may be brought into the same straight line with the rest of the tube.

Keeping this joint hot, a place about an inch from it on the tube a is warmed, and the piece of 1/4-inch tubing previously prepared is sealed on at that point. The joint is then well annealed and allowed to cool.

The tube a is now cut at such a place that when b is inserted in the open end the point will come near the end of the constriction of a, as shown in c. Care is taken to get a clean square cut. The side tube is now cut off about an inch from the main tube and corked. Tube b is sealed into the open end of a, in the same way as a was sealed into the large tube, and the joint carefully annealed.

Discussion.—As in the first method, the secret of success lies in getting a square joint, and having the inner tube leave the outer one at nearly right angles. All the remarks about annealing, lumps, etc., made under the previous method apply here.

This method may be applied in sealing a small tube into the end of a large one, the latter being either drawn to a cone and cut off at the desired diameter, or else given a rounded end like a test-tube and a hole the proper size blown in the center of it. A suitable thick-walled bulb is to be blown on the small tube, as in the case described above. This method is also used in making the Kjeldahl trap (a, Fig. 13), the small tube to be inserted being first drawn, the thick bulb blown at its point of union with the main tube, and then the small tube bent and cut. The large bulb is best made with rather heavy wall, being either blown in the middle of a tube, and one piece of the tube drawn or cut off, or else made on the end of a tube. In the latter case a drop of glass must be put on the point where the joint is to be, so as to get a hole of the proper size with enough glass around it to prevent it from growing larger when it is heated. The author prefers to blow the bulb in the middle of the tube, draw off one end of the bulb, and blow out the desired hole where the tube was drawn off. The whole bulb must generally be reheated and blown a little at the end of the process, and well annealed.

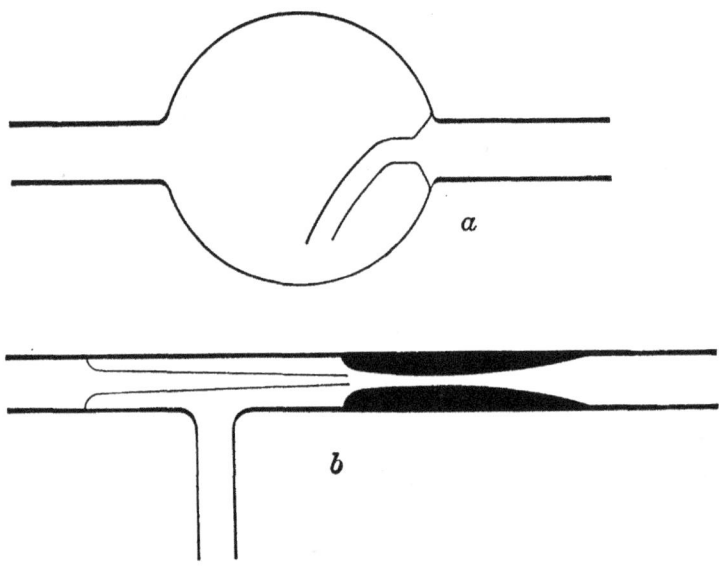

Fig. 13.—*a*, Kjeldahl trap; *b*, suction pump on smaller tubing.

The suction pump can also be made on 1/4-inch tubing, and one joint saved if desired, by constricting the tube to form the raceway for the water and air, as shown in *b*, Fig. 13. (See page 10 for method.) But it is more difficult to make a square joint on such small tubing.

CHAPTER V

MODIFIED METHODS AND SPECIAL OPERATIONS

CAPILLARY TUBING

This is commonly used in many forms of apparatus for gas analysis, and one is often called upon to join two pieces or to make a tee on it. The methods are nearly the same as with other tubing, except that more care and patience are required. The work must be done much more slowly on account of the thickness of the walls, and open ends of the tube must always be enlarged before joining them to anything. This is best done by carefully sealing the end and then blowing, with several suitable reheatings, to form a pear-shaped bulb as in *a*, Fig. 14. The end of this is then heated and blown off, and the piece is ready to be joined to another similar end, or to a piece of ordinary tubing if desired. The joints are best not blown too much, as thick walls shrink very slowly. Much may be done by gently pushing the tube together or pulling it apart in the flame, to remove lumps and irregularities. It is necessary that the bore of the joint be approximately that of the main tube, and care must be taken that the latter is not constricted at the point where the joint begins.

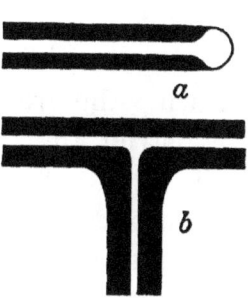

FIG. 14.—Capillary tubing.

Especial care must be taken to warm the tube slowly when starting and cool it slowly when through, as the thick walls frequently crack if not carefully handled. For this reason the whole neighborhood of the joint must be heated somewhat so that there may not be stresses set up between the heated and unheated portions.

In making the tee (b, Fig. 14) the inability to blow the joint makes itself decidedly felt, but if the side tube is properly enlarged as previously described, a good joint can be made by alternately pulling and pushing on the end of the side tube, and shrinking well.

Very fine capillary tubing should be blown with a rubber bulb instead of the mouth, so as not to get moisture into the tube. The rubber bulb may also be used to advantage on some of the coarser capillary tubing.

When a bulb is to be joined to a piece of capillary tubing, the joint is preferably made before blowing the bulb, and will then be taken up a little way on the bulb during the process. Care must of course be taken not to constrict the capillary; the pear-shaped bulb blown on the end (a, Fig. 14) may well extend back a little further than usual into the tube so as to prevent this. If a bulb is required in the middle of a capillary tube, the latter is usually best cut and a piece of ordinary tubing of suitable size sealed in to provide material for the bulb.

GLASS ROD

Joints, tees, etc., in glass rod are made on the same principle as in tubing, except that of course they cannot be blown, and regularity must be obtained by accumulating a small mass of uniformly heated glass, and then drawing it to a suitable rod, on the same principle as Exercise No. 1.

Great care must be taken in heating and cooling this, as in the case of the capillary tubing, and for the same reasons.

By joining pieces side by side, pressing with carbon plates or a plate and a rod, and other suitable manipulations, stirrers, spatulas, and other objects may easily be made from rod, and its manipulation is relatively easy on account of the fact that one does not have to worry about the bore of the tube. But the same general rule about not having thick and thin spots in contact, and making all changes in diameter on a taper if possible instead of abruptly, applies here. Thick pieces will cool and contract at different rates from thin ones, and cracks are likely to develop where they join. Work which has been formed with any tool must always be heated to the softening point afterward before allowing it to cool in order to remove the stresses caused by the contact of the tool with the hot glass.

When it is necessary to join a piece of rod to the side of a piece of tubing, the end of the rod is made very hot while the wall of the tube at the spot desired is heated to just below the softening temperature. The rod can then be pressed into firm union with the tube and drawn a little to remove the excess of glass without deforming the tube.

MENDING STOPCOCKS

Mending the Plug.—The plug of the stopcock occasionally falls out and is broken. If the break is in the main part of the plug, nothing can be done except to search for a spare plug of suitable size and grind it to fit, as described below. If only the little cross-piece at the end is broken off, it can easily be replaced. In most ordinary stopcocks the plug is solid, but the little handle is hollow. What has been said above regarding care in heating and cooling glass rod applies with especial force here. It is usually best to wind the whole of the plug with several thicknesses of asbestos cord, leaving bare only the end where the handle is to be joined. This diminishes the danger of cracking the plug by too rapid heating, and also makes it more comfortable to hold. A piece of rather thick-walled tubing of suitable diameter is chosen, drawn out so as to have a suitable taper (taking care to heat enough of the tube so that the capillary tail has good wall-thickness and strength), and then a corresponding taper is drawn to form the other side of the handle. The result is shown in Fig. 15, *a*. The capillary tail is now heated and bent back to form a handle which will be in the same straight line as the axis

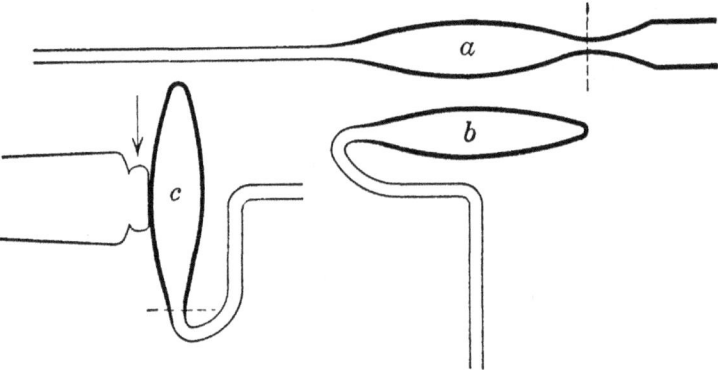

Fig. 15.—Stopcock plug.

of the plug (*b*, Fig. 15) and the main part of the tube drawn off at the dotted line, making a neat seal at that point. The broken end of the plug is now slowly warmed in the smoky flame, the heat gradually increased by a gentle stream of air from the bellows, and the point at which this handle is to be attached finally brought to the temperature at which the glass flows freely. In the mean time, the little handle has been warmed almost to the softening point. It is now quickly pushed into place (*c*, Fig. 15), taking care that its axis is parallel to the hole in the plug, and then drawn away from the plug just enough to make a graceful neck instead of the bulging one indicated by the arrow in the figure. With a fine pointed flame the little tail is now drawn off at the point indicated by the dotted line (*c*, Fig. 15) and the whole carefully annealed. If necessary, the handle can be blown a little before the tail is removed. Local heating and blowing at the point where the handle joins the plug is often necessary in order to make a smooth job.

Regrinding.—This is sometimes necessary to make stopcocks tight, when the grinding has not been properly done in the factory. For this, a very little fine flour of emery or carborundum is the best and quickest. If this is not at hand, some clean sand may be ground in an agate mortar, and if possible sieved. Only material which passes the 100-mesh sieve should be used. It will be ground still finer in the process. For the final polishing, a little infusorial earth or even kaolin will do.

The surface to be ground is moistened with water and dusted over with a little of the abrasive. The plug is now inserted in the stopcock, and turned with a gentle pressure. This turning should be in the same direction for several revolutions, then in the opposite direction for several more revolutions, etc. As the abrasive becomes finer during the grinding, a little more may be added if necessary. In general, only a little grinding will be required, and one small pinch of carborundum or emery will be ample. The beginner usually grinds too much, and with too coarse material. As the grinding surface becomes dry, water is added drop by drop, and the grinding continued until the abrasive seems to be reduced to an impalpable powder, most of which has been squeezed out of the stopcock. The two surfaces in the stopcock are usually grinding upon each other at this stage, and inspection will show whether the contact between them is uniformly good. If not, the grinding must be continued with a little fresh abrasive. If contact appears to be good, the surfaces are ground together for a little with practically no abrasive, so as to polish them, and the joint is then washed out and tested.

In grinding in a new plug to replace a broken one, the plug selected should have practically the same taper as the seat into which it is to be ground, and should be a very little too large. Care must be taken to so distribute the abrasive material as to grind mostly on the places where the plug fits tightly.

Sealing on a New Tube.—It frequently happens that one of the tubes of the stopcock is broken off close to the cock itself, and a new one must be joined to the stub of the old one. With care, this may often be successfully done even where the break is within 1/4 inch of the stopcock. The first step is to clean and dry the stopcock, remove the plug, cork the open ends of the stopcock sleeve and the other tube, and wind a couple of layers of asbestos cord carefully over the sleeve and the most of the corks which close it. A suitable tube, having as near as possible the same diameter and wall strength as the one broken off, is selected and a piece the desired length cut off. The broken end of the tube on the stopcock is now squared off as well as possible, by cutting or by heating and drawing off the projections, and the new tube sealed on, usually with the first method (Exercise No. 1). If the break is very close to the stopcock, very little reheating and blowing can be done, on account of the danger of getting the stopcock sleeve out of shape, and the work must be heated very slowly to prevent cracking. The main reliance is then placed on making a good joint when the tubes are brought together, and then drawing out this joint a little, at once, to get an even wall.

CLOSED CIRCUITS OF TUBING.

In some pieces of apparatus closed circuits of circular or rectangular shape are required. A similar problem is involved in apparatus like the ordinary Soxhlet extractor, where a small tube is joined to the side of a large one, bent to form a siphon, and attached again to a continuation of the original large tube. The difficulty in all such cases is to provide for the contraction taking place as the last joint cools. If part of the circuit has the shape of the letter S, or is a spiral, the natural springiness of the glass will take care of this. If not, the side of the circuit opposite to the joint and parallel to it must be heated also, the two being finally heated together to the softening point after the joint is completed, and then allowed to cool together.

To make the last joint, the rest of the tube is made in approximately the desired form, the two pieces which are to be joined to make the last joint being just enough out of the desired position to allow them to pass one another. The final joint is preferably made in the middle of a straight piece of tube, not at a tee. The two pieces which are to be joined are bent so as to just pass each other, marked at the right point with the glass-knife, and cut there, preferably with a small bead of hot glass. One or both of these tubes are now warmed to the softening point in such a place that the tubes can be made to meet properly, and the two cut ends pressed together. They are now warmed in the flame, and joined together, either by simultaneously warming the opposite side of the circuit or some other suitable part, so as to allow the two ends to be pushed together again after they are softened, or by gently touching the places that do not unite with a hot bead of glass, and using the glass to fill up the crack where the ends do not quite meet. Care must be taken not to leave knots or lumps of glass in the finished joint, and the latter should be well reblown, and if necessary left as a small bulb or enlargement, rather than have it have too thick walls.

SPIRALS

Spirals of glass tubing are probably best made free-hand before the blow-pipe, unless one has a great many of them to make, and extreme accuracy is desired. To begin with, a piece of tubing of the desired size (say 3/16 inch in diameter) and a convenient length (about two feet) is selected, one end closed, and a right-angle bend made

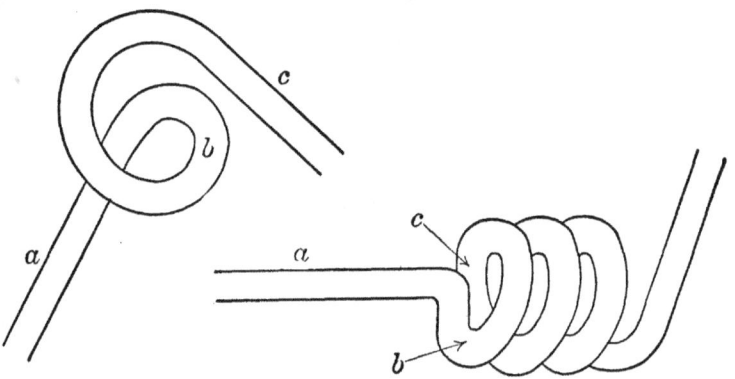

FIG. 16.—Making a spiral.

about six inches from the closed end. Holding the closed end in the left hand and the long open one in the right, the spiral is begun. The short closed end is to be parallel to the axis of the spiral, and preferably in that axis. Using a moderate-sized flame, of somewhat yellow color, and taking care to heat the whole circumference of the tube, the long open end is wound little by little into a spiral having the short end a (Fig. 16) as an axis. The bend at b, where the tube changes from the radius to the circumference of the circle, must be rather short, but the tube must not be flattened or constricted here.

Especial pains is to be taken with the first turn of the spiral (*b* to *c*, Fig. 16), as the shape of this determines the diameter of the whole spiral, and serves as a guide for the rest of the turns. The winding of the tube is best accomplished, after a portion has been softened, by slowly turning the short end *a* a little about its own axis, while the long open end remains where it was. This winds the tube into a spiral, just as if there were a solid cylinder in the center of it, and this cylinder was being turned about its axis, and was winding up the soft glass upon its circumference. As the cylinder is not actually there, the curve of the turns must be carefully estimated by the

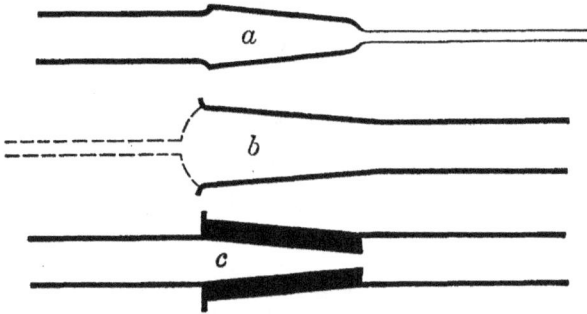

Fig. 17.—Ground joint.

eye, so that the spiral may be uniform and moderately smooth. When the original piece of tube has been used up, another piece is sealed on to the open end, and the operation continued as far as may be required.

GROUND JOINTS

It is sometimes required to join two pieces of tubing end to end, by means of a ground joint. Whenever possible, a regular sealed joint should be used instead of this ground joint, as it is quicker to make, and more certain to be tight. Where a ground joint is necessary, however, it is best made in the conical form shown in *c*, Fig. 17. If the wall of the tube to be used is not very thick, it is thickened by collecting glass as for a bulb on the ends of two tubes (Exercise No. 6), and drawing to form cones of suitable shape (a and b, Fig. 17) and of such relative sizes that a will slip about half way into b. In order to make a straight and give it the proper angle, it may be rolled when hot, upon a hot plate of carbon. Blowing during this rolling is often helpful to remove depressions. After b has been drawn to nearly the proper size and shape, it may be smoothed by the use of a small carbon rod, held inside it at a slight angle, or better by the use of a truncated hexagonal pyramid of carbon, whose edges have the proper slant to make the inside of the cone right. The proper taper for both these cones is the same as that used in stopcocks of similar size. The hexagonal carbon can easily be made by carefully filing down an electric light carbon, and finally impregnating it with paraffin or beeswax, and is extremely useful wherever a conical surface has to be formed from the inside of a tube.

The tail is allowed to remain on piece a, as a sort of guide in grinding, and should therefore be in the axis of the tube and have rather thick walls. Grind with emery or carborundum, as described under a previous head. (Regrinding plug for stopcock.) If many such joints are to be made, it will pay to have a little sleeve of brass made with the proper taper, and rough down the plug a in it to about the proper size, while b is roughed down by means of a brass or iron plug having the same taper. This prevents excessive grinding of one-half of the joint in order to remove a defect in the other half, and is the method commercially used in making stopcocks.

SEALING IN PLATINUM WIRE

Very often it is necessary to seal platinum wire into the wall of a tube. Professional glass-blowers usually use a special sort of glass ("Einschmelzglas") which is usually a lead glass, and is made of such composition that it has the same or practically the same coefficient of expansion as platinum. A little globule of this glass is sealed into the tube in such a way that it joins the platinum to the glass of the tube. To do this, the small globule of special glass is fused on the platinum wire at the proper point and the tube into which the wire is to be sealed is heated and a small tail drawn out at the point where the wire is to be inserted. The lump of the special glass should be from 3/32 to 1/8 inch in diameter, and the tail drawn on the tube

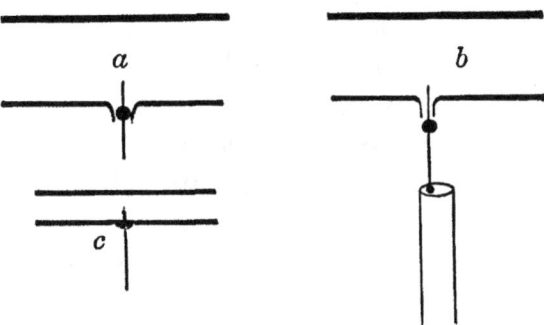

Fig. 18.

should have a slightly less diameter at the point (about 1/8 inch or less from the tube) where it is cut off. There are now two ways of sealing in the wire. (1) The wire with the globule of glass is placed inside the tube and the latter revolved until the end of the wire sticks out of the cut tail (*a*, Fig. 18). The latter is now gently heated, and the two glass surfaces fused together, taking care to use only the end of the hissing flame, if the special glass contains lead. (See Chapter I, page 1.) The whole circumference of the tube is then heated and annealed carefully. (2) The end of the wire which is to be outside the tube is attached to the end of a thin scrap of glass, by heating the glass and thrusting the wire into it a very little way. Using this piece of glass as a handle, the wire is inserted in the cut tail (*b*, Fig. 18) and the globule brought near to the end of the tail. (If the main tube is cold, it must of course first be warmed.) With the end of the hissing flame, as in the first method, the globule of glass is melted and the end of the tail softened. The wire is now pushed into place, the handle removed by heating the end and withdrawing it, and the tail reheated a little if necessary to make it shrink back into line with the walls of the tube. The whole circumference of the tube is heated at that point and annealed as usual.

The use of this special glass is not absolutely necessary if the platinum wire is small (1/4 millimeter or less in diameter), and in fact it is often better in such cases not to use it, unless the apparatus is to be subjected to a very high vacuum. On small tubes, especially, it is undesirable to use the special glass, as a lump of it will usually cause the tube to crack on cooling. When such glass is not at hand or is not to be used, the procedure is altered somewhat. The tail which is drawn out is very fine, having only a sufficient diameter so that when it is cut off the wire can be inserted in it. Such a fine tail is readily made by heating a small spot on the tube, touching it with a warm platinum wire, removing from the flame and drawing out the tail with the wire. After cutting off the tail the wire is inserted in it, being held on a scrap of glass as in the previous case, and the wire and tail heated until the latter shrinks back into line with the walls of the tube. If too great shrinkage occurs, the place may be blown out gently after reheating. Thus the wire is sealed through the wall of the tube without changing the thickness of the latter, and consequently without developing undue stresses at that point. Such

MODIFIED METHODS AND SPECIAL OPERATIONS 55

a joint must of course be carefully reheated and annealed. With fine platinum wire there is very little risk of the tube cracking if care is taken to avoid formation of any lump and to reheat the whole circumference of the tube at that point.

Any glass adhering to the end of the platinum wire, where the scrap of glass was sealed on for a handle, may be removed when the glass has cooled by crushing it carefully with a pair of pliers.

SEALING VACUUM TUBES

Tubes which have been evacuated usually are sealed off while they are still connected to the vacuum pump. The connection should be through a small, rather thick-walled tube. When this is to be sealed, it is slowly heated toward the softening point. As the glass just begins to soften, the air-pressure will force it in, and care must be taken that the softening is uniform over the whole circumference of the tube. As the shrinking goes on, the tube is gently drawn out to make a thick-walled cone at that place, and the end is drawn off as soon as the tube is sealed. The principal point to be guarded is the thickness of the walls of the cone, and uniform heating. A thin place or a hot place will give way under the air-pressure and be sucked into the tube.

CLOSED TUBES FOR HEATING UNDER PRESSURE

(*Carius method for determination of the halogens and sulphur.*) In this case the tubing used must have thick walls (usually about 3/32 inch) to withstand the pressure. Its external diameter is usually about 3/4 inch. One length will usually make two tubes of standard length for the cannon furnace. Especial care must be taken in heating and cooling it on account of the thick walls. A length is gradually warmed in the center, finally heated at that point until soft, drawn out, cut apart and annealed. Taking one of the pieces, the cone is carefully heated and shrunk, as in Exercise 4, until its walls are as thick as those of the main tube. A flame with a little tinge of yellow should be used for this operation to prevent devitrification (page 2), as the thick glass shrinks slowly. The tail is now drawn off and the whole end heated and gently blown several times to make a rounded end, like a test-tube, with walls as thick as those of the main tube. This must be carefully annealed. It is more important that the walls be thick than that the end be nicely rounded: it may indeed be left somewhat conical in shape.

At a point about two inches from the open end of the tube, it is slowly warmed and finally heated to the softening point. Grasping the open end with a pair of crucible tongs, it is cautiously pulled out, a little at a time, usually during rotation in the flame, to make a constriction of moderate wall-thickness, but of sufficient internal diameter to admit the tube containing the substance. After annealing this, cooling and cleaning the tube, the acid and salt are introduced (the former by means of a long-stemmed funnel) and the tube is inclined and rotated about its axis so that the acid wets its surface about half way up from the bottom. The substance is now weighed out in a piece of thin-walled glass tubing, closed at one end, and about two inches long. Inclining the large tube at a suitable angle, the small one is introduced, closed end first, and allowed to slide down the walls of the large tube until it reaches the place where the acid has wet the tube. Here it will stop, and if the tube is kept inclined during the rest of the operation it will roll around inside the tube at this point and thus not get down where any acid is likely to get into it and produce any pressure by decomposing it before the open end of the tube is sealed. Now the tube is held in an inclined position, taking care that the acid does not reach up to the substance, the constricted portion cautiously warmed and shrunk. It is finally shrunk and drawn out into a somewhat elongated cone, with walls as thick as the rest of the tube, and when this is accomplished the end of the cone is sealed and the waste piece drawn off. Anneal with great care, and cool in such a position that the acid cannot reach the hot glass. The shrinking of this cone takes a good deal of patience, and is one of the most important parts of the process. If the walls are left too thin, the tube may burst when heated, and the whole labor is lost. If care is taken, the same tube can be used for a number of determinations. until it becomes quite short.

INDEX

Annealing glass, 4, 24

Bellows, 4
Bending glass, 8
Blowing glass, 13, 19, 20, 21, 24, 29, 31
    with a rubber tube, 22
Blowpipe, 4
Bulb at end of tube, 28
    in middle of tube, 32
    very large, 32
Bulbs, string of, 33

Capillary tube, drawing on larger tube, 9, 54
    tubing, working, 43
Carius method, tubes for, 55
Closed circuits of tubing, 48
    tubes, for heating under pressure, 55
Collecting glass for bulb, 29, 31, 32
Constricting a tube, 10
Crystallization of glass, see Devitrification.
Cutting glass, 7, 25

Devitrification, 1, 2
Drawing out a tube, 9, 18, 19, 27

Flanging a tube, 11, 14
    tool, 11

Gas-washing tube, 35
Glass, annealing, 4, 24

Glass, bending, 8
    blowing, 13, 19, 20, 21, 24, 29, 31
    collecting for bulb, 29, 31, 32
    cutting, 7
    defects, 2
    grinding, 47
    hard, 1
    knife, 7
    lead, 1
    qualities desired, 1
    rod and tube, joining, 45
    rod, working, 44
    shrinking, 18, 19, 22, 26
    soft, 1
    working temperature, 1, 13, 19, 27
Grinding stopcock or joint, 47
Ground joints, 51

Handle on stopcock, mending, 45
Hard glass, 1
Holding tube, 13, 14

Insertion of tube through another, see Sealing a tube through another tube.

Joints, ground, 51
Joining rod and tube, 45
    tubing end to end: first method, 16
    second method, 20

Joining tubes of different diameters, 25
    a new tube to a stopcock, 48

Kjeldahl trap, 41

Lead glass, 1
Lump of glass, removed, 18, 19, 20, 21, 24, 26, 30, 38

Platinum wires, sealed into glass, 1, 52
Position for glass-working, 5
Pressure, tubes for heating under, 55

Quality of glass, 1

Rod, glass, working, 44
Rotation of the tube, 13, 19
Rounded end of tube, 35, 38
Rubber tube used for blowing, 22

Sealing a tube through another tube, 35, 39

Sealing vacuum tubes, 55
Shrinking glass, 18, 19, 22, 26, 31
Side tube, blowing, 22, 25
Soda glass, 1
Soft glass, 1
Spirals, making, 50
Stopcocks, mending, 45
Suction pump, 39, 42
Sulphur dioxide tube, 28

"Tail" of glass, drawing out, 9, 54
    removed, 30, 35
Tubes, closed, for heating under pressure, 55
"Tee" tube, 22
    on capillary tubing, 43
    small side tube on a large tube, 24

Vacuum tubes, sealing, 55

Working temperature of glass, 1, 13, 19, 27

Recipes
for
Flint Glass Making

By a
British Glass Master and Mixer

Being Leaves from the Mixing Book of Several Experts in the Flint Glass Trade

Containing up-to-date Recipes and Valuable Information as to Crystal, Demi-crystal and Coloured Glass in its Many Varieties

It Contains the Recipes for Cheap Metal suited to Pressing, Blowing, etc., as well as the most costly Crystal and Ruby

British Manufacturers have kept up the Quality of this Glass from the Arrival of the Venetians to Hungry Hill, Stourbridge, up to the Present Time

The Book also contains Remarks as to the Result of the Metal as it left the Pots by the respective metal mixers, taken from their own Memoranda upon the Originals

SECOND EDITION

"THE POTTERY GAZETTE" OFFICES
8 BROADWAY, LUDGATE HILL, E.C.

First Edition, *July*, 1900.
Reprinted, *April*, 1907.

CONTENTS.

	PAGE
Notes by the Compiler	iii
Ruby Glass Recipes	1-5
German Metal Recipe	6
Cornelian Recipes	7
Sapphire Blue Recipes	8
Crysophis Recipes	9
Opal Recipes	10-13
Turquoise Blue Recipes	14, 15
Gold Colour Recipes	16
Green Recipes	17
Malachite Recipes	18
Black Recipe	19
Canary Recipes	19
White Opaque Glass Recipes	20
Sealing Wax Red Recipes	21
Flint Glass Recipes	22-25
Achromatic Glass Recipe	26
Paste Glass Recipe	26
White Enamel Recipe	27
Firestone Recipe	27
Dead White Recipe	28
Agate Recipes	28
Canary Recipes	29
Index	30

NOTES BY THE COMPILER.

Repeats are given of more than one recipe, so that the mixer may acquaint himself how to use up his cullet or to vary his mixture to suit his requirements.

The cost given of the cheap metal is based on the cost of materials some year or two ago, but it is approximately correct at the present time.

The sand used in most of the recipes is French (Fontenbleu), except in some old forms, when it was Isle of Wight; and the soda supplied by a Northwich firm.

Colouring should generally be about half put into the batch and the other half reserved until the long proof has been taken off, when it can be added to or diminished to suit furnace or the weather.

The sand in the *crystal* should be washed and calcined. In the commoner metal it is used as it arrives; still the quality is greatly improved by the first process.

Many of the finest colours containing cryolite should be worked immediately it is plain.

In using brass, it is necessary to insure correctness that it should always be the same. Brass differs in its composition.

The greatest care should be taken in the purity of all material, and the greatest care should be taken that everything is clean and free from dust and dirt.

In all these colourings allowance must be made throughout this book for the state of the furnace, weather, purity of sand and material, etc.

July, 1900.

RUBY.

	Cwt.	qrs.	lb.	oz.
French Sand (Fontenbleu)	2	2	20	0
Red Lead	2	2	20	0
Saltpetre	0	0	18	0
Antimony	0	0	9	0
Manganese	0	0	2	0
Gold in Solution, "Purple Precipitate of Cassius"	0	0	0	$1\frac{1}{2}$
Nitric Acid	0	0	0	1
Muriatic Acid	0	0	0	4

"Mix and then add the gold; when fine, work into lumps. There used to be much difficulty in preparing this purple precipitate, but it is now an article of commerce. Mind it is pure."

ANOTHER RUBY.

Sand	32 lb.
Red Lead	36 ,,
Saltpetre	16 ,,
Manganese	$1\frac{3}{4}$ oz.
Antimony	2 ,,
Gold (in Solution)	1 ,,

ANOTHER RUBY.

Saltpetre	$9\frac{1}{2}$ lb.
Sand	18 ,,
Red Lead	23 ,,
Red Lump Cullet	11 ,,
"Waste Last Pot"	6 ,,
Manganese	$2\frac{1}{2}$ oz.
Antimony	1 ,,
Gold (Precipitated)	5 drams.

"Very good pot as ever was made. Beautiful colour. Put colour in the middle of the pot."

ANOTHER RUBY.

Saltpetre	16 lb.
Sand	32 ,,
Red Lead	36 ,,
Manganese	1¾ oz.
Antimony	2 ,,
Gold (Precipitated)	1 ,,

"This mixture turned immediately it was put into the lear. Fill the pot for ruby a little at a time, and watch that it does not ferment. It does not require above twenty hours to fine; and mind the pot does not get too hot. When it is worked into lumps, put it into the lear with some fine ashes. Keep it turned often, and when a dark ruby get it down the lear; if it be not all dark, it will right itself in the plating. The metal from the pot should be a light straw colour."

A RUBY FROM COPPER.

	Cwt.	qrs.	lb.
Sand	4	2	0
Pearl Ashes	1	0	24
Red Lead	0	3	16
Carbonate of Lime	0	0	25
Phosphate of Lime	0	0	5
Red Tartar (Crude Tartar)	0	0	5
Borax	0	0	5
Oxide of Tin	0	0	$3\frac{1}{2}$
Red Oxide of Copper	0	0	$2\frac{1}{2}$

"Give it all the air you can, compatible with getting it plain; too great heat is against it."

FLINT FOR USING WITH THE RUBY FOR COATING (on pages 2 and 3).

Sand	64 lb.
Lead	72 ,,
Saltpetre	32 ,,
Manganese	1¼ oz.

"Charge your pot with two-thirds and 'dragade' it; next morning charge again with the rest and the ladings, and add 4 oz. manganese and 8 oz. of antimony."

A GERMAN METAL (Flint).

	Cwt.	qrs.	lb.
French Sand - -	- 10	0	0
Refined Soda - -	- 1	2	0
Common Soda Ash -	- 3	2	0
Lime Spar - -	- 1	0	0
Fluor Spar - -	- 0	2	0
Nitrate of Soda - -	· 1	0	0

"Sand unburnt and unwashed. This mixture is given to form the body of some of the following coloured metals, and is called 'German cullet or body'. These delicate colours require great care."

CORNELIAN, OR ALABASTER.

German Cullet (page 6) -	35 lb.
Black Ash - - -	15 oz.
Nitrate of Soda - -	8 ,,
Manganese - - -	1 ,,

"This way very good."

ANOTHER CORNELIAN.

	Cwt.	qrs.	lb.	oz.
German Cullet (page 6) -	4	1	0	0
Black Ash - - -	0	0	11	0
Nitrate of Soda - -	0	0	7	0
Manganese - - -	0	0	0	15

"Very good."

SAPPHIRE BLUE.

German Cullet (page 6)	14 lb.
Black Ash	5½ ,,
Nitrate of Soda	3½ ,,
Copper Scales	2 oz.

"Very good."

ANOTHER SAPPHIRE BLUE.

	Cwt.	qrs.	lb.
German Cullet (page 6)	3	1	0
Black Ash	0	0	11
Nitrate of Soda	0	0	8
Copper Scales	0	0	3¼
Blue Cullet	1	0	0

"Filled an overtaker. Very good."

ANOTHER SAPPHIRE BLUE.

	Cwt.	qrs.	lb.
German Cullet (page 6)	2	3	0
Cullet	1	2	0
Nitrate of Soda	0	0	7
Copper Scales	0	0	2½

"Very good."

CRYSOPHIS.

	Lb.	oz.	drs.
German Cullet (page 6)	14	0	0
Black Ash	0	5½	0
Nitrate of Soda	0	3½	0
Uranium (Oxide)	0	2	0
Green Oxide of Chrome	0	0½	8
Sulphide of Copper	0	0	3

"Very good."

ANOTHER CRYSOPHIS.

	Cwt.	qrs.	lb.	oz.
German Cullet (page 6)	2	2	0	0
Crysophis Cullet	1	3	0	0
Saltpetre	0	0	11	0
Oxide Uranium	0	0	2½	0
Sulphate of Copper	0	0	0	10

"Very good."

OPAL.

	Cwt.	qrs.	lb.	oz.
Sand	2	0	0	0
Lead	0	3	0	0
Ash	0	2	0	3
Plaster of Paris	0	2	0	0
Lime Spar	0	0	14	0
Manganese	0	0	0	3
Nitrate of Soda	0	0	7	0
Arsenic	0	0	0	8

ANOTHER OPAL.

	Cwt.	qrs.	lb.	oz.
Sand	2	2	0	0
Lead	1	1	0	0
Ash	1	0	11	0
Fluor Spar	0	1	24	0
Felspar	0	1	24	0
Saltpetre	0	0	12	0
Manganese	0	0	0	5

"Very good."

ANOTHER OPAL.

Sand	100 lb.
Lead	80 ,,
Ash	28 ,,
Saltpetre	30 ,,
Calcined Bones	20 ,,
Antimony	4 oz.

ANOTHER OPAL.

	Cwt.	qrs.	lb.	oz.
Sand	3	3	12	0
Cryolite	0	3	16	0
Lead	0	1	5	0
Soda	0	3	16	0
Nitrate of Soda	0	0	13	0
Arsenic	0	0	2	0
Manganese	0	0	0	3

"BEST" OPAL.

Sand	600 lb.
Soda	240 ,,
Felspar	225 ,,
Fluor Spar	225 ,,
Arsenic	6 ,,
Cryolite	5 ,,
Nitrate of Soda	65 ,,

ANOTHER OPAL.

	Cwt.	qrs.	lb.	oz.
Sand	1	3	20	0
Cryolite	0	1	22	0
Ash	0	0	20	0
Red Lead	0	0	20	0
Soda	0	1	22	0
Nitrate of Soda	0	0	8	0
Arsenic	0	0	1	0
Manganese	0	0	0	$1\frac{1}{2}$

ANOTHER OPAL.

	Cwt.	qrs.	lb.	oz.
French Sand	6	1	0	0
Lead	4	0	22	0
Ash (Pot)	3	1	6	0
Fluor Spar	1	1	12	0
Felspar	1	1	12	0
Saltpetre	0	1	8	0
Manganese	0	0	0	14

ANOTHER OPAL.

Sand	150 lb.
Soda	60 ,,
Nitrate of Soda	5 ,,
Barytes	13 ,,
Arsenic	8 oz.
Manganese	5 ,,

"This was changed into blue by adding oxide of cobalt, 4 oz., and about 40 lb. of blue cullet."

ANOTHER OPAL.

Sand	700 lb.
Red Lead	470 ,,
Ash (Marshall's)	370 ,,
Felspar	152 ,,
Fluor Spar	152 ,,
Saltpetre	36 ,,
Manganese	14 oz.

ANOTHER OPAL.*

Sand	600 lb.
Soda (B., M. & Co.)	240 ,,
Felspar	225 ,,
Fluor Spar	225 ,,
Arsenic	6 ,,
Cryolite	5 ,,
Nitrate of Soda	65 ,,

TURQUOISE BLUE.

Sand	100 lb.
Red Lead	80 ,,
Saltpetre	28 ,,
Ash	28 ,,
Calcined Bones	18 ,,
Arsenic	4 ,,
Brass Filings	1½ ,,

ANOTHER TURQUOISE.

	Cwt.	qrs.	lb.
Batch	0	1	12
Turquoise Cullet	3	0	0
Oxide of Iron	0	0	1
Copper Scales	0	0	2
Opal Cullet	0	1	12

"Very good, very soft, not regular batch; work immediately it is fine; last instruction important."

ANOTHER TURQUOISE.

Batch (A, page 22)	504 parts.
Plaster of Paris	14 ,,
Fluor Spar	24 ,,
Felspar	24 ,,
Arsenic	6 ,,
Black Oxide of Copper	9 ,,
Black Oxide of Cobalt	$2\frac{3}{4}$ oz.
Phosphate of Lime	9 parts.

ANOTHER TURQUOISE.

Opal Batch (* page 13)	28 lb.
Arsenic	4 oz.
Zaffer	$1\frac{1}{2}$,,
Brass	12 ,,
Cullet (Turquoise)	70 lb.

GOLD COLOUR.

	Cwt.	qrs.	lb.
Sand	1	1	0
Soda	0	2	4
Spar	0	0	25
Calcined Oats	0	0	1

"Good and right."

ANOTHER GOLD COLOUR.

	Cwt.	qrs.	lb.
Amber Cullet	3	0	0
Batch (A, page 22)	0	3	0
Calcined Oats	0	0	$\tfrac{3}{4}$

"Very good. You may calcine your own oats in the lear or furnace. Sometimes ground and sifted coke is used, but it is not so pure a carbon."

DARK GREEN.

Cullet	112 lb.
Batch (A, page 22)	336 ,,
Crocus Marcus	13 ,,
Copper Scales	4 ,,
Oxide of Copper	3 oz.

"Very good."

ANOTHER GREEN (Common).

	Cwt.	qrs.	lb.	oz.
Green Cullet	1	0	0	0
Batch (A, page 22)	0	2	24	0
Oxide of Iron	0	0	4	0
Copper Scales	0	0	1	0
Oxide of Copper	0	0	0	1

GREEN FOR MALACHITE.

	Cwt.	qrs.	lb.	oz.
Green Cullet	1	0	0	0
Green Siftings	0	3	0	0
Batch (A, page 22)	0	2	24	0
Oxide of Iron	0	0	4	0
Copper Scales	0	0	1	0
Oxide of Copper	0	0	0	2

"Very good."

BLUE FOR MALACHITE.

	Cwt.	qrs.	lb.	oz.
Batch (A, page 22)	3	2	0	0
Blue Cullet	1	0	0	0
Zaffer	0	0	5	0
Manganese	0	0	0	8

BLACK FOR MALACHITE.

Use Batch A, page 22, and treat it as Crystal Batch on page 19, and this will produce a black metal which will incorporate with the blue and green metal above, and will anneal safely.

"These three colours will work mixed from the pots; one gathered upon the other and manipulated on the 'marver,' then pressed, or melted in again in the furnace and blown; anneal them well."

BLACK.

Batch (Crystal Batch)	56 lb.
Flint Cullet	56 ,,
Manganese	12 ,,
Iron Scales	3 ,,

"A good pot of black which was not greasy."

COMMON CANARY BATCH.

Sand	1,100 lb.
Ash	336 ,,
Spar	264 ,,
Lead	100 ,,
Nitrate of Soda	40 ,,
Arsenic	6 ,,
Oxide Uranium	$4\frac{1}{2}$,,

CANARY.

Batch (as above)	14 lb.
Uranium	1 oz.
Sulphate of Copper	$\frac{3}{4}$,,

"This gives the proportion of colourings to 14 lb. batch."

ANOTHER CANARY.

Batch (as above)	336 lb.
Canary Cullet	100 ,,
Oxide Uranium	14 oz.

WHITE OPAQUE GLASS.

Sand	100 parts.
Calcined Ash	50 ,,
Slacked Lime	16 ,,
Oxide of Tin	60 ,,

ANOTHER WHITE OPAQUE GLASS.

Sand	100 parts.
Minium	78 ,,
Calcined Ash	30 ,,
Nitrate of Soda (Crystals)	8 ,,
White Oxide of Tin	62 ,,

"These will be interesting, as they are from a very old book of recipes."

SEALING WAX—RED—(Experiment).

Saltpetre	3 lb.
Lead	6 ,,
Sand	9 ,,
"Raw Brass"	1 ,,
"Colclother of Vitriol"	1 ,,
Red Tartar	1 ,,

"Was a wax red, but faded. Wanted working when plain, probably."

ANOTHER WAX—RED.

Cullet (out of the above experiment)	20 lb.
Added—Red Tartar	2 ,,
Brass	8 oz.
Colcothar of Vitriol	1 lb.

"This produced a good wax red after being in the furnace twelve hours. The colour was throughout very good."

FLINT (A)—(A very cheap Metal).

	Cwt.	qrs.	lb.	oz.
Sand	12	2	0	0
Alkali (B., M. & Co.)	4	1	0	0
Ash (Marshall's)	0	3	18	0
Spar	1	0	8	0
Barytes	0	3	14	0
Nitrate of Soda	0	2	18	0
Arsenic	0	0	5	0
Manganese (about)	0	0	1	14

"Costs about 2s. 8d. per cwt. into pot. (Evaporation 13 to 15 per cent.)"

A BATCH (B)—(A little more costly).

	Cwt.	qrs.	lb.
Sand	12	0	0
Soda (B., M. & Co.)	4	1	0
Lead	0	1	0
Spar	1	0	0
Nitrate of Soda	0	2	0
Saltpetre	0	2	0
Arsenic	0	0	2
Manganese	0	0	$1\frac{1}{4}$

"Costs about 3s. 2d. per cwt."

FLINT GLASS (Crystal and Demi).*

Refined Pearl Ashes	76 lb.
Saltpetre	10 ,,
Lead	200 ,,
Sand	260 ,,
Manganese	4 drs.
Arsenic	8 lb.

* Nearly every house in Britain uses different proportions, but we give a variety. The costs will be apparent to the mixer.

ANOTHER CRYSTAL FLINT GLASS.

	Best.	Common.
Sand	560 lb.	500 lb.
Lead	330 ,,	350 ,,
Ash	160 ,,	150 ,,
Saltpetre	60 ,,	30 ,,
Arsenic	1 ,,	1 ,,

ANOTHER CRYSTAL FLINT GLASS.

Sand	520 lb.
Lead	360 ,,
Ash	160 ,,
Saltpetre	35 ,,

"Colouring."

ANOTHER FLINT (C).

	Cwt.	qrs.	lb.	oz.
Sand	12	2	0	0
Alkali (B., M. & Co.)	4	1	0	0
Ash (Marshall's)	0	3	18	0
Spar	1	0	8	0
Barytes	0	3	14	0
Nitrate of Soda	0	2	18	0
Arsenic	0	0	5	0
Manganese	0	0	1	14

"Costs about 3s. 7¼d. per cwt. Very good. Evaporation 13 to 15 per cent."

ANOTHER FLINT (D).

	Cwt.	qrs.	lb.
Sand	12	0	0
Soda (B., M. & Co.)	4	0	0
Nitrate of Soda	1	0	0
Ash	0	1	0
Lead	0	1	0
Spar	1	0	0
Arsenic	0	0	7
Manganese	0	0	1

"Costs about 2s. 10d. per cwt. Evaporation 13 to 15 per cent."

FLINT (a good blowing Metal).

	Cwt.	qrs.	lb.
Sand	12	0	0
Alkali	4	0	0
Lead	1	0	0
Saltpetre	1	0	0
Spar	1	0	0
Ash	0	2	0
Arsenic	0	0	5
Manganese	0	0	2
Cobalt	11 grs.		

"Costs about 4s. 6d. per cwt."

ACHROMATIC GLASS.

Lead	500 lb.
Sand	600 ,,
Ashes (Refined)	180 ,,
Saltpetre	60 ,,
Manganese	7 oz.
Antimony	3 ,,

"This is the right quantity."

PASTE GLASS.

Furnace let out, and pots allowed to cool.

Refined Pearl Ashes	97 parts.
Lead	200 ,,
Sand	260 ,,
Saltpetre	10 ,,
Manganese	$\frac{1}{2}$ oz.
Arsenic	12 ,,

"The paste was very good. The foundering was kept twenty-four hours longer, but the furnace was kept little hotter than a working furnace, and was then let out gradually, being kept for twelve hours little better than a pot arch. This paste was perfect to the bottom of the pot when broken up."

WHITE ENAMEL.

Sand	50 lb.
Saltpetre	20 ,,
Lead	50 ,,
Arsenic	$4\frac{1}{2}$,,
Antimony	$\frac{1}{2}$,,

"A very good pot of white, and worked clear."

FIRESTONE.

Sand	125 lb.
Saltpetre	30 ,,
Lead	150 ,,
Arsenic	$7\frac{1}{2}$,,
Antimony	$\frac{1}{2}$,

"This was a pot of very good firestone."

DEAD WHITE (for Moons).

Sand	28 lb.
Lead	21 ,,
Ashes	11 ,,
Arsenic	2½ oz.
White Cullet	200 lb.

"A very good pot. Worked clear and well."

WHITE AGATE.

Sand	24 lb.
Lead	25 ,,
Saltpetre	15 ,,
Calcined Bone Ash	1 ,,
Arsenic	4 ,,

ANOTHER AGATE.

Sand	67 lb.
Lead	54 ,,
Ash	20 ,,
Saltpetre	11 ,,
Arsenic	6 ,,
Bone Ash	10 ,,

"Very good."

CANARY.

Sand	$5\frac{1}{4}$ parts.
Lead	$3\frac{1}{2}$,,
Ash	$1\frac{1}{8}$,,
Saltpetre	$\frac{1}{2}$,,
Oxide Uranium	$\frac{1}{358}$,,

"No arsenic. No manganese. Well mixed in a clean harbour. As a rule it takes 5 oz. of uranium to the cwt. Don't use the blacks from the iron when you use the cullet. This is a very tender colour to make."

CANARY ENAMEL.

To Blacks (Cullet)	100 lb.
Use Chromate of Lead	$\frac{3}{4}$,,

"Dissolve any quantity of lead (sugar of lead) in warm water; dissolve chromate of potash in warm water; put the one into the other by degrees, stirring all the while with a glass rod till no more precipitate falls; strain off the liquid and wash the precipitate which is chromate of lead; filter it, and it is fit for use. Don't use the chromate of lead of commerce; it is not pure."

INDEX.

Achromatic glass, 26.
Agate, white, 28.
Alabaster, 7.

"Best" opal, 11.
Black, 19.
Black for malachite, 18.
Blue for malachite, 18.
Blue, sapphire, 8.
Blue, turquoise, 14, 15.

Canary, 19, 29.
Canary batch, common, 19.
Canary enamel, 29.
Common canary batch, 19.
Common green, 17.
Cornelian, 7.
Crysophis, 9.
Crystal flint glass, 23.

Dark green, 17.
Dead white (for moons), 28.

Enamel, canary, 29.
Enamel, white, 27.

Firestone, 27.
Flint, 22, 23, 24, 25.
Flint for using with the ruby for coating (on pages 2 and 3), 5.

German metal, A (flint), 6.

Glass, achromatic, 26.
Glass, flint (crystal and demi), 22, 23, 24, 25.
Glass, paste, 26.
Gold colour, 16.
Green, common, 17.
Green, dark, 17.
Green for malachite, 18.

Malachite, black for, 18.
Malachite, blue for, 18.
Malachite, green for, 18.

Opal, 10, 11, 12, 13.
Opal, "Best," 11.
Opaque glass, white, 20.

Paste glass, 26.

Red sealing wax, 21.
Ruby, 1, 2, 3.
Ruby from copper, 4.

Sapphire blue, 8.
Sealing wax, red, 21.

Turquoise blue, 14, 15.

White, agate, 28.
White, dead (for moons), 28.
White enamel, 27.
White opaque glass, 20.

www.ingramcontent.com/pod-product-compliance
Lightning Source LLC
Chambersburg PA
CBHW081016040426
42444CB00014B/3226